TO BE A
PARATROOPER

Gregory Mast and Hans Halberstadt

Zenith Press 10/07

First published in 2007 by Zenith Press, an imprint of MBI Publishing Company, Galtier Plaza, Suite 200, 380 Jackson Street, St. Paul, MN 55101 USA

Zenith Press titles are also available at discounts in bulk quantity for industrial or sales-promotional use. For details write to Special Sales Manager at MBI Publishing Company, Galtier Plaza, Suite 200, 380 Jackson Street, St. Paul, MN 55101 USA.

To find out more about our books, join us online at www.zenithpress.com.

About the authors:

Gregory Mast enlisted in the Marine Corps in 1978 and was commissioned in 1983. Following his active military service he worked in the defense industry on classified projects, as a web communications specialist at design studios, as a freelance graphic designer, and has owned a traditional Irish pub. He and his wife live in San Jose, California.

Hans Halberstadt studied documentary film in college and later took up writing, authoring or co-authoring more than fifty books. Most of his books have been on military subjects, especially U.S. special operations forces, armor, and artillery. He has also written extensively about farming and railroads. Halberstadt served in the U.S. Army as a helicopter door gunner in Vietnam. He and his wife, April, live in San Jose, California.

Unless otherwise noted, all photographs are courtesy of the U.S. Army.

Cover: U.S. Air Force pararescuemen from the 31st Rescue Squadron perform a static-line jump out of a C-130 Hercules aircraft over a body of water near Kadena Air Base, Japan, August 29, 2006. The 18th Wing and the 353rd Special Operations Group are conducting a mass-casualty exercise to test the rescue and emergency care capabilities of Kadena Air Base. *Department of Defense photo by Staff Sgt. Steven Nabor, U.S. Air Force*

Frontispiece: After a few rides down the cable, most students manage to hold a good, tight body position during opening shock. *Gregory Mast*

Title Page: Students land at Fryar Drop Zone following a mass exit with combat equipment. They lower their ALICE packs and M1950 weapons cases on the HPT line at about two hundred feet above ground level. The T10's anti-inversion netting is clearly visible on the canopy in the foreground. *Gregory Mast*

Table of Contents: BAC students must make one "night" jump in order to graduate. During the summer months, the night jumps are often twilight or sunset jumps, due to long daylight hours and a compressed training schedule. Here, two students prepare to land at Fryar Drop Zone. *Gregory Mast*

Back Cover, left: Students at BAC will spend hours sitting on the benches in McCarthy Hall during jump week. Bad weather or aircraft maintenance issues will occasionally create delays as well. *Hans Halberstadt* **Top right:** The T10D parachute, currently in use as the standard parachute for mass tactical drops, is a direct descendent of the parachute that carried paratroopers into Normandy on D-day. The T10 has been in use since the 1950s, with modifications. The U.S. Army is developing a replacement for the aging T10 series, the advanced tactical parachute system (ATPS), which is expected to be in service by 2010. *Gregory Mast.* **Bottom right:** A BAC student exits a Lockheed C-141 over Fryar Drop Zone. The static line is stowed on the parachute pack by retainer bands, which keeps the static line from becoming fouled or tangled before exiting the aircraft. As the jumper leaves the door, the static line is pulled out of the retainer bands and fully extends, pulling the deployment bag from the parachute pack.

ISBN-13: 978-0-7603-3046-3
ISBN-10: 0-7603-3046-8

Library of Congress Cataloging-in-Publication Data
Mast, Gregory.
  To be a paratrooper / text by Gregory Mast ; photography by Hans Halberstadt.
    p. cm.
  ISBN-13: 978-0-7603-3046-3 (softbound)
  ISBN-10: 0-7603-3046-8 (softbound)
  1. United States. Army—Parachute troops—Training of. 2. Fort Benning (Ga.) I. Halberstadt, Hans. II. Title.
  UD483.M37 2007
  356'.16650973—dc22
                            2006032317

Editor: Steve Gansen
Designer: Cindy Laun

Printed in China

CONTENTS

Preface 6

Acknowledgments 8

Introduction 9

ONE   **Get Ready: Preparation for Basic Airborne Course** 22

TWO   **Reporting In: Stand Up** 30

THREE   **Ground Week: Hook Up** 36

FOUR   **Tower Week: Check Equipment** 58

FIVE   **Jump Week: Stand By** 80

SIX   **Life After the Basic Airborne Course: Go** 120

Index 142

Preface

So you want to go to jump school? Congratulations. Upon graduation you will join a proud military tradition whose history of heroism and courage dates back to World War II. Your jump wings will earn you membership in an elite club, for whom jumping out of an airplane is just another way to get to the office. First, you have to spend three fun-filled weeks at the U.S. Army's Fort Benning, Georgia, facility earning those wings. The purpose of this book is to assist in preparing you for that adventure.

Preparation for the Basic Airborne Course (BAC) is both a physical and mental process, because physical and mental toughness are traits of the airborne soldier world-wide. Parachute operations are high risk and are not the domain of cowards or crybabies. There are those who think that the only things that fall from the sky are bird crap and fools. If you believe that, then jump school is not for you. Fortune favors the brave, and not everybody has what it takes to become a paratrooper.

Apprehension about exiting an aircraft in flight, before it has come to a complete stop at the terminal, is normal. That is what separates the airborne soldier from the foot soldier, or "leg," the ability to overcome normal fear and step out into the slipstream. Those who stay inside the airplane will never know the thrill each time the canopy blossoms. Courage is not the absence of fear but the ability to act in the face of fear. And courage is the stock-in-trade of the paratrooper.

Some may question your sanity for wanting to jump out of a perfectly good airplane. No offense intended to the aviation community, but there is no such thing as a perfectly good airplane. The Lockheed C-130 Hercules cargo aircraft has often been defined as 250,000 rivets flying in loose formation. After a long, turbulent flight, you might even consider clawing your way to the front of your stick, or group of paratroopers on the same jump, just to get out of the airplane ten seconds faster.

Physical training prior to checking in at Benning is an absolute necessity for most students. Unless you are a Recon Marine or a Navy SEAL, the physical demands of Airborne School will present a challenge. The cadre has two jobs: one is to teach you how to get from the airplane to the ground without killing yourself. The other is to weed out the physically weak, because they are a threat to themselves and to others around them. There is no excuse for lack of physical conditioning when a student arrives, and those who fail the physical fitness test that is administered on the first day of ground week receive little sympathy.

Airborne school is the beginning of your journey, a milestone rather than the destination. It doesn't get easier after graduation, as the jumps are much more difficult out there in the fabled "real world." The danger remains constant and ranges from the mild inconvenience of your airsick buddy puking on you while still in the aircraft, to the serious risk of physical injury upon landing, and up to the possibility of the ground terminating your plummet—and your life—in the event of canopy failure. The risk of injury and death is present before the first shot is fired. It is difficult, dangerous work, and the paratroopers bought and paid for their reputation for tenacity on the battlefield.

The Basic Airborne Course is a gateway to exciting and exotic opportunities. Airborne qualification is a basic requirement for rangers, Green Berets, Delta Force, and other special operations forces. Jump school is a rite of passage, and those who successfully complete the course can be justifiably proud of their wings.

In one of the most widely recognized images from World War II, General Eisenhower addresses members of Easy Company, 502nd Parachute Infantry Battalion, on June 5, 1944. In fewer than twelve hours, the 101st Airborne Division would be committed to combat for the first time, parachuting into Normandy to spearhead the D-day invasion of France.

The maroon beret has been a symbol of airborne forces since World War II. Long an unofficial uniform item in the U.S. Army, it gained official recognition in the 1980s. Only soldiers who are assigned to airborne units are authorized to wear this distinctive headgear. *Hans Halberstadt*

A member of A Company, 2nd Battalion, 3rd Special Forces Group, Fort Bragg, North Carolina, performs a pivot poised exit on a night jump with oxygen and equipment, at 25,000 feet above Roosevelt Roads Naval Air Station, Puerto Rico. The Basic Airborne Course is a prerequisite for assignment to special operations forces.

Jump school is physically challenging, and students are expected be in excellent condition prior to arriving at Fort Benning. Each day is filled with demanding training and rigorous physical exercise. Students will do hundreds upon hundreds of pushups during the Basic Airborne Course.

Opposite: The basic parachutist badge, or "jump wings," is the reward for completing the Basic Airborne Course at Fort Benning, Georgia. Since World War II, jump wings have been one of the most prized qualifications in the U.S. armed forces. *Gregory Mast*

Acknowledgments

Authoring any book of nonfiction is not a solitary task. This book is no different, and I relied on many people for their experience, knowledge, trivia, and war stories (which are mostly nonfiction). It is largely due to their generosity that I was able to finish this project, and it is to them that I dedicate this book. I can only hope that I have done justice to their story.

First, I would like to acknowledge the 1st Battalion (Airborne), 507th Infantry, and collectively thank the officers and soldiers of that battalion for their assistance, patience, and tolerance during my visits to Fort Benning. An observer with a notebook and camera is a pain in the ass, yet every Black Hat instructor took time, a commodity in short supply in a hectic training schedule, to answer questions or offer their real-world experiences when asked. They also went out of their way to make sure that I knew what was going on and how to get there.

Although everyone was exceptionally helpful and outgoing, I would be remiss in not recognizing those who went well beyond the call of simple military courtesy and without whom my time spent at Fort Benning would have been wasted. Maj. Eric Beaty, in his capacity as operations officer for the battalion, coordinated my visits superbly, allowed me unrestricted access to observe training activities, and answered my annoying emails promptly. Capt. Vince Bray, commanding officer of Alpha Company, was generous with his hospitality and time as I followed his company through training, even permitting me to join his company on a run.

The Black Hats are responsible for the future of the airborne, and they execute this responsibility with remarkable professionalism and good humor. Life as an instructor at the Basic Airborne Course is driven by a grinding, never-ending training cycle, and the pace is relentless. Only the most dedicated and knowledgeable noncommissioned officers (NCOs) can make the grade as Black Hats. To that end, I would like to give special thanks to a few who went the clichéd extra mile in helping me with this project. So to Sgt. 1st Class George Box, Chief Petty Officer Toby Michleski, USN, Staff Sgt. Mark Gigowski, Staff Sgt. Michael Reid, Staff Sgt. Jeremy Garcia, Staff Sgt. Shannon Hill, Staff Sgt. Joshua Humphries, Staff Sgt. Robert Contratto, Staff Sgt. Samuel Brinkley, Staff Sgt. Jeremy Dillard, Staff Sgt. Ryan Dittachio, Staff Sgt. Clint Hoover, and Sgt. Jeremiah Kuepper, USMC, I offer my gratitude for your assistance and instruction and wish you each the best of luck.

I would also like to thank 1st Sgt. Ed Howard, USA (Ret.), for his help with historic and technical questions about the Basic Airborne Course. Ed was a Black Hat and a company first sergeant at BAC and has spent years studying the history of the U.S. Army. He has a unique expertise in the history of jump school and airborne forces. Ed recently started a new career as a high school teacher but still found time to answer my emails, even if he had to do it at four in the morning. Thanks, Ed, and I look forward to your books.

Hans Halberstadt, my co-author, has been an excellent mentor and teacher, as well as a good friend. Hans was responsible for getting me this project, so send your complaints to him, as this mess is his fault. Thanks, Hans.

This is the point in most acknowledgements for the "and finally" paragraph, where the author's spouse gets recognition for putting up with him when he has been a raging maniac during the process of writing the book. I know this is customary, but, truth be told, the order is backward, and those who have tolerated the author's stressed-out antics should be listed first. So, as a humble servant of tradition, I would like to thank Vernie, my wife of twenty-two years and counting, for her support, tolerance, encouragement, and love, without whom my life would be poorer. Thanks, Vernie. By the way, have I mentioned my next project?

Introduction

Fort Benning, Georgia, is synonymous with the United States Army Infantry and Airborne training programs. Today, Fort Benning is home to the U.S. Army Infantry Training Brigade, U.S. Infantry School, Ranger Training Brigade, Airborne School, and School of the Americas, making it one of the busiest training facilities in the U.S. Army. It is also home to operational units, including the 3rd Brigade, 3rd Infantry Division (Mechanized) and the 75th Ranger Regiment, as well as combat-support units. On average, approximately fourteen thousand students graduate from the Basic Airborne Course every year.

Located in west-central Georgia, just south of Columbus, Fort Benning was established in 1918 as Camp Benning, but did not come of age until the start of World War II. The camp was named after Henry L. Benning, a Columbus native and general in the Confederate Army. At the time the camp was established, Columbus was a small town in which the memory of the Civil War was still strong and Confederate sympathies ran high. During the Civil War, Columbus ranked just behind Richmond in the production of munitions and war materials for the South's war effort. Large portions of the city were burned to the ground during Sherman's March to the Sea. The last significant land battle of the War Between the States was fought at Columbus, when the city was attacked on Easter Sunday, 1865, by a Union force under the command of Gen. James Wilson. The city is a treasure-trove of museums and historical sites for the military-history enthusiast.

Fort Benning did not receive permanent status until 1940, when the first permanent quarters and facilities were constructed to accommodate an army undergoing wartime expansion. It was during this time that the U.S. armed forces underwent a massive transformation in size, doctrine, and technology. During the years between the two world wars, the bureaucratic inertia of the War Department resisted change, even as the world changed radically before their eyes. It took the German blitzkrieg of 1939 to jolt the War Department into a crash program

Fort Benning, illustrated to scale in red, is located south of Columbus. One of the largest and busiest training facilities in the U.S. Army, Fort Benning is home to 1st Battalion (Airborne), 507th Infantry, the unit responsible for basic parachute training.

Gen. Henry L. Benning, Confederate States of America, is the namesake for Fort Benning. A native of Columbus, Georgia, he personally raised the 17th Georgia Infantry at the start of the Civil War. Following the Battle of Antietam, he was promoted to brigadier general and took command of a brigade that later participated in the Battles of Gettysburg and Chickamauga.

Fort Benning underwent massive expansion of its facilities in the early 1940s in order to train an expanding army. Shown here are an M3 Lee medium tank and a trainee of the armored forces completing the course at Fort Benning in early 1942.

The 250-foot towers have been landmarks at Fort Benning since 1941. The towers were not acquired from Coney Island but were constructed specifically for the army. Students are dropped from the towers to learn how to control their canopies. *Gregory Mast*

Sketch from Leonardo da Vinci, dated 1483. Leonardo wrote, "If a man is provided with a length of gummed linen cloth with a length of twelve yards on each side and twelve yards high, he can jump from any great height whatsoever without injury."

to modernize the army. Even so, the country was ill prepared for war when the attack on Pearl Harbor propelled it into World War II.

Fort Benning is huge, encompassing 182,000 acres within its boundaries. Still largely undeveloped, the rolling and forested terrain is dotted with drop zones, landing zones, and firing ranges. Ninety-three percent of the base is in Georgia, while the remainder lies across the Chattahoochee River in Alabama. The soldiers on the base know the Chattahoochee colloquially as the "Chattanasty," in reference to the muddy green color of the river. The climate can be quite pleasant, I am told, but I have no personal experience to verify that claim. Summer is crunch time for the Basic Airborne Course, when the greatest numbers of students attend. This can present a serious, potentially life-threatening problem to those not acclimatized to the heat and humidity, especially during July and August.

The 1st Battalion (Airborne), 507th Infantry, located on the Main Post, is responsible for providing training for the Basic Airborne Course. The battalion area is almost literally in the shadows of the three remaining 250-foot towers located on Eubanks Field, prominent and iconic landmarks dating back to the origin of the U.S. Airborne. The training at Airborne School has changed little since World War II, and this is reflected in many of the traditions of the school. Airborne training was conducted in several locations during and after World War II, including Fort Bragg, but all basic parachute training for the U.S. Army was consolidated at Fort Benning in the mid-1960s.

A SHORT HISTORY OF THE U.S. AIRBORNE PROGRAM

There are many books and films that document the fascinating history of airborne warfare. Most of the traditions of the Airborne are rooted in this history of tenacity, bravery, and heroism. I am including a very brief history of the U.S. Army's airborne program at the request of the cadre at the Basic Airborne Course. It is a common opinion among the Black Hats that far too many students arrive at the course without even a basic grasp of historically significant events that shaped the modern paratrooper. Of course, ignorance of history will not prevent a parachute from opening, but an appreciation of history can provide motivation when the training gets tough.

The concept of delivering soldiers to the battlefield from the sky is centuries old. Many creative military thinkers concocted fanciful schemes to accomplish this task, most composed of wishful thinking and fantasy. Perhaps most notable was Benjamin Franklin's suggestion, more than two hundred years ago, that balloons be used to drop troops behind fortified lines.

The concept of the parachute is even older, with Leonardo da Vinci sketching a pyramid-shaped canopy of wood and linen in the fifteenth century. It is not known if any brave soul undertook a proof-of-concept jump using this device prior to the twenty-first century. In June 2000, Adrian Nicholas, a British citizen, dropped from a hot-air balloon ten thousand feet above the ground using a device constructed of materials that would have been available in 1483, proving that Leonardo had it right after all. Mr. Nicholas did not ride the device all the way to the ground, cutting away to a modern parachute at three thousand feet, but impact would have been survivable and not much worse than that of a World War II-era parachute.

THE EARLY DAYS

World War I is where the story of the modern airborne had its start. This is when the two key technologies were developed to take the concept from fantasy to reality. The airplane and the parachute were just two of many revolutionary military technologies to emerge from the war, but they happen to be the two that are necessary for airborne operations. Although an ill-conceived parachute operation was proposed near the end of the war, the first true demonstration of the concept would not take place until eleven years after World War I was over.

Colonel Billy Mitchell, having reverted to that rank from brigadier general in 1925, staged the first practical demonstration of dropping combat soldiers from aircraft by parachute in 1929. Six soldiers jumped from Martin bombers over Fort Kelly, San Antonio, Texas, landed safely, and assembled their weapons within minutes. Unfortunately, this feat was overshadowed by Colonel Mitchell's highly publicized court-martial and went largely unnoticed in the United States. It did not go unnoticed elsewhere. The Soviet Union was the most aggressive early adopter of the airborne concept, creating several large airborne formations as well as broadly promoting a civilian sport parachuting program. Italy formed airborne units at the same time as the USSR, but the Italian program was much smaller in scale and scope.

Gen. William "Billy" Mitchell, shortly after World War I. During the war he proposed an airborne operation, but it was not until 1929 that he made one of the first practical demonstrations using American paratroopers. General Mitchell's visionary contribution to the development of airborne forces was overshadowed by his infamous court-martial.

German fallschirmjägers (paratroopers) following the capture of the "impregnable" Fort Eben-Emael in Belguim, May 1940.

Orrigional Member
Co A; 503rd
October

5 Row (S, R)
1. Hofland, Erie
2. Moore
3. Stamerancy, Ralph
4.
5. Hilke, Williams
6. Houk, Dang
7. Butler (B-503)
8.
9. Carpenter, John (A.
10. Tupper
11. Sprecher, Clyde
12.
13.
14. Nelson

Lt. Cry
Lt. Dammers - 5
Lt. Pratt
Lt. Caple

3rd Row (S, R)
1. Stryker (RP.)
2. Sinclair (RP.)
3. Botonely, John
4. Stark, Eby
5. Orruk, Pete
6. Simpson, LeRoy F. (A.C.)
7. Kennedy, Joe - (B-503)
8. Abbott, Elmer (504)
9. Martin
10. Cano (B-503)
11. Strobic, Al
12.
13. Vernon, John - (A.C.)

2nd Row (S-R)
1. Peterson
2. O'Brien
3. Bigart
4. Scalpall, Robert - (B-503)
5. Marshall,
6. Nelson,
7. Betz,
8.
9. Aycock, Roy (O.C.S)
10. Smith (B-503)
11. Buchholtz (quit later O.C.S.)
12. Dixon
13. Morley, John D.
14. O'Day
15.

4th Row (S, R)
1. Penland, Jr. - (A.C.)
2. Freeman, Howard
3. Nelson, John - (A.C.)
4. Rhoden

12

Original members of Company A, 503rd Parachute Battalion, in a photo dated October 1941. *Major Thomas Simpson, USMCR (Ret.)*

Backside of the photograph of members of Company A, with handwritten names. *Maj. Thomas Simpson, USMCR (Ret.)*

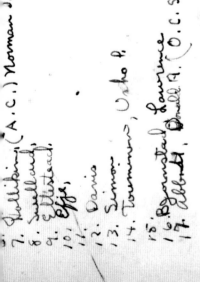

The Germans were the first to use airborne troops in combat. Preceding the invasion of Norway in April 1940, *fallschirmjägers* (paratroopers) seized key airfields, in what is now considered a standard mission for airborne forces. In May 1940, the *fallschirmjägers* spearheaded the German invasions of Belgium and Holland, most famously capturing the "impregnable" fortress of Eben-Emael with eighty-five soldiers, delivered by parachute and glider. It was about this time, in April 1940, that the War Department (predecessor to the Department of Defense) approved a plan to form a test platoon of airborne infantry.

In July 1940 the Test Platoon was formed under the command of 1st Lt. William T. Ryder, who has the honor of being regarded as the U.S. Army's first paratrooper. A group of forty-eight enlisted men was selected from a volunteer pool of more than two hundred soldiers to form the platoon and step into the pages of history. It may be difficult to comprehend now, in our age of extreme sports, just how radical the airborne concept was to the U.S. Army at the time. The United States was playing catch-up, and the Test Platoon literally had to make it up as it went along, improvising equipment and training.

The platoon was initially billeted at Lawson Army Airfield, at Fort Benning, with early phases of its training taking place in New Jersey. The first jump took place at Lawson Field on August 13, 1940, with Lieutenant Ryder the first to exit the Douglas C-33, the predecessor of the Douglas C-47. A lottery was held to determine the jump order, and Pvt. William N. "Red" King was the first enlisted man to exit after Lieutenant Ryder. Private King had placed second in the lottery, but to his good fortune the lottery winner refused to jump once in the door. The platoon made its first mass jump on August 29.

The army began forming airborne combat units shortly thereafter, starting with the 501st Parachute Battalion, followed quickly by other parachute battalions and regiments. The rapidly expanding units created a requirement for a centralized training facility, and Fort Benning was designated as such in May 1942. Since that time, the U.S. Army has developed its basic parachute training doctrine at Fort Benning. It is worth noting that the army placed a very high value on its airborne formations. One measure of that is that the monthly jump pay was $55, at a time when the average soldier was paid $17 a month in base pay. This financial incentive drew many volunteers.

WORLD WAR II

The U.S. Army's first combat jump took place during Operation Torch, the Allied invasion of North Africa. The 509th Parachute Infantry Battalion (PIB) boarded their aircraft in England, with the mission of capturing two airfields around Oran, Morocco, following a long flight over Spain. The mission was a bit of a fiasco, with navigation and communications problems causing the battalion to become scattered from Gibraltar to Tunisia. The 509th captured the airfields despite these problems, and they went on to make several additional drops in support of Operation Torch.

The next operation was the invasion of Sicily in July 1943, known as Operation Husky. The 82nd Airborne Division made its first combat jumps in another operation that was plagued by navigational errors, communications problems, bad weather, and friendly-fire incidents. This operation forced the U.S. Army to make changes to the airborne training program and to refine its tactical doctrine. The 82nd Airborne Division and the 509th PIB also participated in Operation Avalanche, the invasion of Italy, in September 1943.

Airborne forces were critical to the success of Operation Overlord, more commonly referred to as D-day. On June 6, 1944, a massive Allied force launched the invasion of Europe on the beaches of Normandy. Parachute and glider operations were mounted in what was at the time the largest airborne operation ever. The 82nd and 101st Airborne Divisions were again widely scattered, and many units were dropped far from their intended drop zones. Countless acts of individual courage and heroism took place during the desperate and dark hours prior to the first landing craft hitting the beach. Paratroopers earned their reputation for initiative, bravery, and improvisation in operations like D-day, where, despite heavy casualties and overwhelming odds, they accomplished critical missions.

The next major airborne operation of the war was Operation Market-Garden in September 1944. The operation was bold, bordering on reckless. Some thirty-five thousand paratroopers and glider troops were dropped up to one hundred miles behind enemy lines to capture a series of bridges that would allow for a rapid advance into occupied Holland. They were to hold the bridges for up to seventy-two hours, following which the plan called for the airborne forces to be relieved by the advancing British Second Army. The 101st Airborne Division was dropped around Eindhoven and was relieved on schedule.

Paratroopers on a training jump over England in 1944, prior to the invasion of Normandy. Note the jump boots and distinctive uniform of the airborne soldier.

The 82nd was dropped around Nijmegen, encountered stiff resistance, and was relieved three days later than scheduled. The British 1st Airborne Division and the Polish 1st Independent Parachute Brigade were not as lucky. They were trapped at Arnhem for nine days, where nearly fifteen hundred were killed in action and nearly sixty-five hundred were taken prisoner. This is a very brief summary of a very complex operation, which has provided enough material for several books alone. The story of Operation Market-Garden is dramatized, with some degree of accuracy, in the film *A Bridge Too Far.*

Both the 82nd Airborne and 101st Airborne Divisions fought heroically in the Battle of the Bulge, during the brutally cold December of 1944. The 101st is remembered for its refusal to surrender when surrounded at Bastogne, holding out against vastly superior forces until it was relieved by General Patton's Third Army.

In Operation Varsity, the last major airborne operation of the war, the 17th Airborne Division and the British 6th Airborne Division crossed the Rhine and jumped into Germany in March 1945. The operation is widely considered to be the most successful airborne operation of World War II.

Airborne operations in the Pacific Theater of World War II are less well known and were on a smaller scale than operations in Europe. The 503rd PIB made combat jumps in New Guinea in 1943 and 1944, and the 11th Airborne Division made several combat jumps during the invasion of the Philippines.

COMBAT JUMPS SINCE WORLD WAR II

The Korean War began on June 25, 1950, when North Korea invaded South Korea in a surprise attack. The United States made two combat jumps during this conflict, both by the 187th Regimental Combat Team. The first was made on October 20, 1950, in North Korea to cut off an avenue of retreat from Pyongyang. The second was made on Easter Sunday, 1951, in South Korea.

Airborne divisions and brigades served in Vietnam during the length of the conflict. However, there is only one recorded combat jump during that war: 845 members of the 173rd Airborne Brigade jumped in support of Operation Junction City in February 1967. Both the 82nd and 101st Airborne Divisions served in Vietnam, primarily in the role of light infantry and airmobile forces.

During Operation Urgent Fury, October 1983, rangers from the 75th Ranger Regiment jumped into the airfield at Point Salines, Grenada. The 82nd Airborne participated in the operation but did not jump.

The army made three combat jumps during Operation Just Cause in December 1989. The 2nd Battalion, 504th Parachute Infantry Regiment, seized the Torrijos Airport in Panama. The 75th Ranger Regiment conducted the other two jumps.

Three combat jumps have been made in support of Operation Enduring Freedom in Afghanistan. On October 19, 2001, the 3rd Ranger Battalion, 75th Ranger Regiment, made a night jump to secure an airfield in Kandahar, Afghanistan. In November 2001, B Company, 3rd Ranger Battalion, conducted a combat jump in a remote region in Afghanistan to establish a forward staging base. In February 2003, elements from the 2nd Ranger Battalion and the 82nd Airborne Division conducted a jump in western Afghanistan that remained classified for more than a year.

(Left) U.S. Air Force colonel Steve Weart prepares for an airdrop with the 173rd Airborne Brigade into northern Iraq during Operation Iraqi Freedom.

Paratroopers darken the sky over Holland during Operation Market-Garden, September 1944.

Members of the 187th Regimental Combat Team, the "Rakkasans," prior to making a combat jump in Korea, October 1950.

President Lyndon B. Johnson decorates an officer from the 82nd Airborne Division during his visit to Vietnam in October 1967.

A member of the 82nd Airborne Division assists a Cuban national who was wounded during Operation Urgent Fury, the invasion of Grenada, in October 1983.

Geronimo—medicine man, warrior, and leader of the Chiricahua Apache, around 1895. Named "Geronimo" by the Mexican army (his Apache name was Goyathlay), he fought both the Mexican and U.S. Army for decades, as both countries encroached on his tribal lands. At one point, he evaded a force of five thousand soldiers-one-fourth of the U.S. Army at the time-for a year. He surrendered in 1886, and with him, the last major force of independent Indian warriors to oppose the U.S. government's occupation of the American West.

On March 19, 2003, during Operation Iraqi Freedom, C Company, 3rd Ranger Battalion, conducted a combat jump into western Iraq. The mission was to secure an airfield in advance of invading coalition forces. On March 26, 2003, the 173rd Airborne Brigade conducted a combat jump onto the Bashur Airfield in northern Iraq.

AIRBORNE TRADITIONS AND HERALDRY: GERONIMO, JUMP BOOTS, AND SILVER WINGS

Elite military units around the world often have unique traditions, dress, and insignia that distinguish them from the ordinary line units. The units cherish and revere these traditions and pass them on from one generation of soldiers to the next, like family heirlooms. The U.S. Army Airborne has its share of customs and traditions, often reflecting a force that was born in a time of crisis and forged in the crucible of battle. Some are whimsical, playful almost, started by high-spirited young men coping with the high-intensity stress of training for combat. That is how the spirit of a famous Apache warrior came to Georgia.

The battle cry of "Geronimo!" has been associated with the American paratrooper since the early days of the airborne program. It captured the imagination of the American public during World War II and remains famous to this day. The image of a paratrooper exiting a C-47 while shouting "Geronimo!" is one of the enduring images from that war and is as American as the flag on his right sleeve. The tale of how an Apache warrior, who made his name fighting the U.S. Army in the 1870s, came to be the unofficial motto of the paratrooper is a story often told in the airborne but is not well known by the general public.

The origin of the Geronimo tradition is typically masculine and military: it was based on a bet and a dare. The generally accepted story is that Pvt. Aubrey Eberhart, of the 501st Parachute Battalion, was the first to shout "Geronimo!" when exiting the door for a jump. He did this to prove to his buddies that he was not afraid, inspired by a Western film by that name they had watched together a few nights prior. Soon many other paratroopers were emulating Private Eberhart, shouting "Geronimo!" during their exits. In fact, the custom became so widespread that it had to be officially prohibited for safety reasons, as paratroopers were neglecting to make sure their main parachute opened after the count of four thousand in favor of shouting "Geronimo!" Still, the tradition lived on, in spite of official disapproval, and today the memory of Geronimo is still honored by paratroopers serving around the world.

Soldiers of 1st Battalion, 509th Infantry, 82nd Airborne Division, conduct operations in support of Operation Just Cause, the invasion of Panama, in December 1989. Their goal was to capture Manuel Noriega.

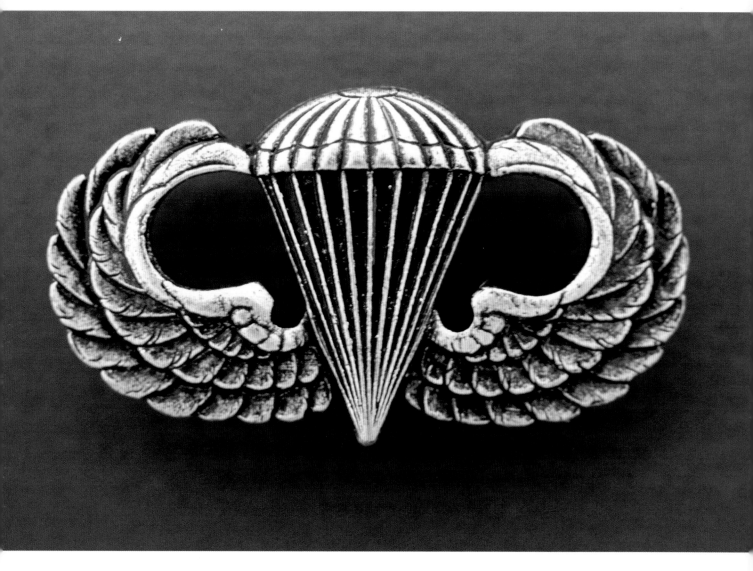

The basic parachutist badge was designed by Capt. William Yarborough, of the 501st Parachute Battalion, in March 1941. There were no distinctive insignia or badges for the newly formed airborne units, so Captain Yarborough was dispatched to Washington, D.C., with authority to create a suitable badge for paratroopers. Captain Yarborough's mission was a success, with the first newly minted jump wings arriving at the 501st less than two weeks later. *Hans Halberstadt*

It was during those early days that another airborne tradition was born, this time out of necessity rather than bravado. The standard-issue combat boots of the time were unsuitable for jump operations, offering insufficient ankle support needed during landing. A special boot was developed for airborne units, one that had a distinctive toe cap and extended well above the ankle. The normal combat boots of the time generally went to just above the ankle and were worn with leggings. Soon, "jump boots" became the envy of the army. Many a barroom brawl has erupted when paratroopers found "legs" wearing unauthorized jump boots. Although most modern combat boots are suitable for parachute operations, airborne troopers still wear jump boots as a distinctive uniform item for dress and parade functions.

Born in the frantic prewar scramble to create parachute battalions, and polished in the desperate battles of World War II, jump wings have come to symbolize more than just an individual paratrooper's airborne qualification, but membership in an elite club. The jump wings that have adorned paratrooper's uniforms for more than sixty years were created almost a year after the War Department authorized the formation of the Test Platoon. The badge was designed by Capt. (later Lt. Gen.) William Yarborough of the 501st Parachute Battalion during a remarkable two weeks in March 1941, perhaps setting a world land-speed record for Pentagon procurement.

Captain Yarborough arrived in Washington, D.C., on March 3, 1941, with the mission of procuring a suitable badge for parachutist qualification. Carrying the authorization of the commanding officer of the 501st PIB and the chief of infantry, he sketched a design for the badge and hand-walked the approval to various officials over a period of one week. The approved design was sent to Bailey, Banks & Biddle Company in Philadelphia for production of the first 350 badges, and on March 14 they were delivered to the 501st PIB at Fort Benning, Georgia. This was a remarkable feat, and one that is not likely to be duplicated in our age of entrenched procurement bureaucracies.

Pvt. Thomas L. Simpson, 1967. Following jump school, he was assigned to the 101st Airborne and deployed to Vietnam with the division, where he would be awarded the Bronze Star for his service with the division. *Maj. Thomas Simpson, USMCR (Ret.)*

Private LeRoy F. Simpson, 1941. He graduated from jump school in November, 1941, a month before the attacks on Pearl Harbor, and was a member of the 503rd Parachute Infantry Battalion. *Major Thomas Simpson, USMCR (ret.)*

FAMILY TRADITIONS

"I went to jump school in 1966. We were assigned to a barracks identical to the one I had been in at Fort Ord. These were the standard World War II, wooden, two-story squad-bay buildings. We heard that the barracks had been condemned and were to be torn down, but the buildup for Vietnam had caused them to be needed. The truth of that rumor could be seen in the poor condition of the buildings. My bunk was on the second floor. The opening for the stairwell in the floor did not have a banister around it. It was merely a hole in the floor with stairs leading down to ground level. My first impression was that it was pretty dangerous, but then I realized that we were there to learn to jump from airplanes!

"Years later, on one of the rare occasions that I talked with my father about his experiences in World War II, we discovered that we had both been assigned to the very same barracks! It was easily distinguishable, because it was the first barracks adjacent to the road that ran down to the airfield and the intersection of the road that ran in front of the airborne barracks. When I told him of my experiences there, he explained that his were a bit different. When he went to jump school in 1941, it was three months long and was more of a commando school than just a jump school. They learned how to blow up trains, bridges, and tunnels."

-Maj. Thomas Simpson, USMCR (Ret.)

ONE

A student on board a Lockheed C-130 before taking off from Lawson Army Airfield is contemplating the upcoming jump, his third of five required to graduate. *Hans Halberstadt*

Get Ready: Preparation for Basic Airborne Course

Recent graduates of advanced infantry training checking into BAC. The majority of BAC students range in age from their late teens to late twenties. Students who come from active-duty and reserve units, as well as cadets, arrive individually. *Hans Halberstadt*

The Basic Airborne Course requirements are simple enough on the surface. First and foremost, you must be a volunteer. No one can be forced into airborne training. You must be in reasonably good physical condition, preferably younger than the age of thirty-five, and be in a suitable military status. Prior to checking into the school, all volunteer students should prepare their mental, physical, and financial fitness in order to meet the challenge of jump school. Preparation can mean the difference between success and failure, between earning your wings or returning to your unit in shame. The one thing that any student has total control over is his or her preparation prior to arriving at Fort Benning.

IT'S ALL IN YOUR MIND

The first issue all potential students must resolve is their desire and commitment to attend the Basic Airborne Course. Jump school demands more than sheer physical strength but inner mental strength as well. A student's level of motivation can make all the difference when coping with the discomfort of training in hellish heat, the continual exhaustion from prolonged physical exertion, and overcoming the normal fear of heights and falling. Inner strength will keep you going long after your muscles have said "no more." Motivation, in this case, begins with the desire to earn jump wings and the willingness to do the hard work necessary to achieve that goal.

One theme that will be stressed throughout this book is that the Basic Airborne Course is a milestone in

Physical preparation is absolutely critical prior to attending jump school. The single greatest reason for failure at BAC is students who are poorly prepared for the strenuous physical demands of the course.

your military career, not the destination. What this means is that earning an airborne qualification is a gateway to other opportunities, such as special forces. It is just the first of many difficult tests, not the final exam. Think of BAC as an entrance examination into a very selective club.

If you have any doubts about your desire to become airborne qualified, you would be well advised to sort them out prior to arriving at Fort Benning. Poorly committed students constitute a sizeable percentage of those who fail the course, wasting their own efforts, the Black Hats' time, and the government's money. Students who are wishy-washy about becoming a paratrooper are one pet peeve of the Black Hats. To be fair, however, students present so many pet peeves for the Black Hats that the cadre could open their own private petting zoo.

PHYSICAL TRAINING:
PRACTICAL ADVICE FOR FATBODIES

On average, 15 to 20 percent of every class fails the Army Physical Fitness Test (APFT) and flexed-arm hang test that is administered on the first morning of training. If it is their first failure, they are recycled to the next class; if it is their second, they are sent home. Another small percentage of students are dropped during the course as physical training (PT) failures. Some of these failures are the result of injury, but the vast majority are due to a lack of physical fitness. One thing should be absolutely clear to any potential BAC student: there is no excuse for arriving in a poor state of physical conditioning. No excuses will be accepted; no sympathy will be given.

The Basic Airborne Course is physically challenging, each day starting well before dawn and filled with hours of exhausting training. However, any motivated student who has a reasonable state of physical fitness and endurance should be able to pass the course, barring injury incurred during training. Students from some active-duty units may find the PT to be much easier than they are accustomed to on a daily basis. Those students who arrive physically unprepared for the rigors of jump school are destined for a rude wake-up call on the first day of ground week.

The morning run or PT session is just the start of a long, physically demanding day. Students are expected to move at double-time, all the time. Unlike many other courses of military instruction, there are no classrooms

Double time, all the time: students at jump school very rarely move at anything slower. Physical training for BAC should emphasize running. *Gregory Mast*

at jump school, where students can rest during the day. Students receive formal instruction while sitting in bleachers, some covered, some not. Students who are in poor physical condition are soon exhausted and cannot keep up with the training. I interviewed many Black Hats to gather information for this book, and to a man they all emphasized the need for students to be physically fit, with an emphasis on running.

Now that I have your attention, or have bored you to death, let's review practical advice for fitness training. Prior to embarking on any physical fitness training program, you should make sure that you are medically qualified to do so. Check with your doctor, if necessary, before you start training. Nothing will wreck your morning faster than an unexpected heart attack while running.

There are many training programs, courses, and guides available. Individual needs may vary, but the end goal remains the same. Select a program that fits your needs and stick with it. A one-size-fits-all approach may work for younger students, but not for older students approaching the age of thirty. The goal of your training program should include, at a minimum, the completion of a five-mile run with a time of forty-five minutes or

faster after conducting thirty minutes of strenuous activity—muscular strength exercises, muscular endurance exercises, calisthenics, and grass drills.

You are the only person responsible for your physical fitness, but that does not mean that training has to be a solitary endeavor. If you can learn to enjoy the training, it becomes much easier. If possible, do not train alone. A running buddy can make a long run much less boring. A training partner keeps you honest. Finally, exercising with others encourages competition and will make you push yourself harder.

Do not train to the minimum standards. Start with the minimums and work up from there. The minimums are the threshold of failure, not the measure of success.

Pay attention to technique. With proper technique, twenty pushups can become forty, with the same effort. As the cliché goes, work smarter not harder. Your brain is a muscle if you bother to use it.

Start your training program early and stick with your program. Discipline plus time equals physical fitness. Older students will have learned that it is much easier to stay in shape than to get in shape. Do not wait until the month before your class begins to start considering your training program.

An important component of military readiness is predeployment preparation for the family members at home when soldiers are absent for training or operations. Life goes on when the service member is away. *Hans Halberstadt*

BASIC AIRBORNE COURSE PREREQUISITES

Commissioned officers, warrant officers, enlisted personnel, and cadets must volunteer for the course and be less than thirty-six years of age on the date of application. General officers; field-grade officers; warrant officers in grades W-3, W-4, and W-5; and enlisted personnel in pay grade of E-5 and above may be considered for a waiver of age when the examining medical officer recommends to the unit commander that such a waiver be granted.

Volunteers must meet the physical qualification for parachute duty established in AR 40-501. Whether male or female, they must pass the Army Physical Fitness Test (APFT) with a score of 180 points (60 points in each event using the 17 to 21-year age-group scale) and meet the height and weight standard IAW AR 600-9.

United States Military Academy (USMA) cadets must complete Cadet Basic Training. Reserve Officers' Training Course (ROTC) cadets must be under scholarship or contracted. Enlisted personnel must have completed basic combat training, One Station Unit Training (OSUT), or other service equivalent training.

APFT will be administered to the students on the first day of the airborne course by 1/507th cadre. In addition to the APFT, the students will be tested on the flexed-arm hang.

Students may not actually do a million pushups at BAC; it only seems that way. Pushups and other exercises are awarded to inattentive, careless, or poorly motivated students as a performance incentive. *Gregory Mast*

FINANCIAL FITNESS: THE HOME FRONT

Solid advice for any service member, whether preparing for deployment or schools, is to get your finances in order prior to shipping out. This is particularly important if you are married or have dependents, because life goes on during your absence. This section is not intended to be a how-to guide but merely a reminder to add these items to your checklist. There are many resources available to help with this planning, from your unit and elsewhere.

If you are married, your spouse may need a power of attorney to deal with financial matters in your absence. Make sure that your family knows the location of important papers or documents.

Have adequate cash available for incidental expenses while attending BAC. Officers and senior enlisted personnel will need cash to pay for their meals or MREs (meals, ready to eat), which are mandatory during jump week.

If you have financial obligations at your permanent duty station, such as rent or car payments, make arrangements so that these do not become distractions while you are at jump school.

SNAFUs with military pay are as old as military service itself. Do not make commitments based on additional allowances, such as jump pay, until you have received those allowances.

PACK YOUR TRASH

The U.S. Army has a very specific packing list for BAC students. Some items may differ for members of other services, so check the current guidelines when packing your gear. Attention to detail is stressed throughout the training at BAC. Checking in with an incomplete or incorrect complement of gear is a guaranteed way to draw the unwanted attention of the Black Hats and could get you returned to your unit. The army's packing list includes:

- Military identification card, in serviceable condition

- Identification tags: one long and one short chain interlaced, with one ID tag per chain. One key, any medical alert badge, and barracks pass (if issued) are allowed to be suspended from the chain.

- Military issue eyeglasses, two pairs, with retainer straps, as required. Civilian eyeglasses are discouraged. Contact lenses are not authorized at any time during BAC (refer to army regulations AR 40-5, *Preventive Medicine*, and AR 40-63, *Ophthalmic Services*).

- Battle dress uniforms (BDUs) or army combat uniforms (ACUs) with appropriate rank, insignia, name tapes, and branch tapes, minimum of three sets. Students from other services will have specific guidelines regarding uniforms and rank insignias.

- One BDU patrol cap or ACU patrol cap or other service equivalent

- Students will not wear the army black, maroon, or green beret prior to graduation. The only authorized head gear is either the ballistic helmet or patrol cap.

- Two web belts and one subdued buckle

- Five brown undershirts or other service authorized undershirts, to be worn with BDUs or ACUs

- Five sets of underwear, five pairs of black or green cushion-soled socks or wear with boots, and five pairs of civilian white athletic socks

- White athletic socks will have no stripes or commercial product markings and will extend beyond the ankles to near mid-calf. Athletic socks that extend only to the ankle are not authorized for wear at BAC.

- Service PT uniform, to include army T-shirt, shorts (summer), sweat top, sweat pants, gloves with inserts, and black wool cap (winter). For those services not issued organizational PT uniforms, such as some navy and air force units, appropriate civilian PT clothes are acceptable. Appropriate colors include solid black, gray, brown, or dark blue attire free of unit and commercial logos.

- Two pairs of standard-issue combat boots for BDUs or hot weather/temperate weather tan boots for ACUs

The gear list for BAC is lengthy, and the items on it will fill a duffel bag. *Gregory Mast*

- Boots should be broken in and must be highly shined. Spit shine is not required.

- Altered boots are not authorized.

- BAC students are not authorized to wear jungle boots, boots with toe and heel caps (e.g., jump boots), or any boots with waffled or rippled soles.

- Civilian running shoes

- Toiletries and shaving gear, three towels, three washcloths, and boot-shining gear

- Two heavy-duty padlocks

- Headband (sweatband) for ballistic helmet; these are available for purchase at Fort Benning.

- During winter season (October-March), black watch cap, and authorized cold-weather jacket (i.e., field jacket with liner, or Gore-Tex-lined waterproof parka)

- Personnel must provide their own military-issue black gloves with liners.

- The Airborne School issues all items of organizational equipment (TA-50) required for airborne training (e.g., helmet, poncho, and canteen).

- Students who require a size extra-large ballistic helmet (Kevlar) and have been previously issued this item and still possess the item are required to bring it to the Basic Airborne Course. Personnel who have not been issued an extra-large ballistic helmet will be provided with one at the course.

DO'S AND DON'TS FOR YOUR ARRIVAL AT BAC

Incoming students will be thoroughly briefed on the standards of military appearance and personal conduct expected from BAC students. Failure to adhere to these standards may result in being dropped from the course. All students will conform to U.S. Army standards of grooming while at BAC, regardless of their branch of service.

Do not get a tattoo within thirty days of reporting to BAC. Students who arrive with new tattoos will be dropped from the course and returned to their units. Students are not authorized to get tattoos while attending BAC.

Dietary supplements are not authorized for use by any personnel attending courses on Fort Benning. These supplements are sold under a variety of brand names, so check the current list of prohibited products before arriving at BAC. Ignorance is no excuse, and possession or use of prohibited supplements could result in Uniform Code of Military Justice (UCMJ) charges.

Tobacco products of any kind are not authorized in the training area. Students with tobacco habits may have to endure up to twelve hours without a smoke break. Now may be a good time to consider kicking the habit.

Mustaches of any kind are prohibited at BAC. Male students will be clean-shaven unless they have a valid medical shaving profile. All students will conform to U.S. Army grooming standards.

Do not wear unauthorized decorations or awards. As stupid as it may sound, students have arrived at BAC wearing ranger tabs when they are not ranger qualified. You are traveling with your military records, so any fraud will be easily detected and punished severely.

Do not arrive late, intoxicated, or both. Students are not authorized to consume alcohol within twenty-four hours of training. There will also be at least one unannounced urinalysis during training. Drug or alcohol violations will result in ejection from the course, with at least an Article 15 as a consolation prize.

Students older than the age of thirty-five are eligible for an age waiver, if they can meet the physical qualifications for the course. Every class has a few "old guys," such as this sergeant first class, a veteran of Operation Iraqi Freedom. *Hans Halberstadt*

THE CHALLENGE OF THE SCHOOL

"Going through the Basic Airborne Course has never been easy. It takes a toll on your body, no matter how well you are prepared. You hit the ground a lot of times, you do a lot of pushups, and there are a lot of very physical demands placed on your body. There is a constant series of impacts and no healing time during the first two weeks of the class, and it wears everybody down."

—Col. Gerald Schumacher, U.S. Army Special Forces (Ret.)

TWO

Recent graduates from advanced infantry training arrive at jump school. They are met by a Black Hat for in-processing and an initial briefing. During the briefing, new students will be given the opportunity to drop out before the course begins. Very few new students accept the offer to quit early. *Gregory Mast*

Reporting In: Stand Up

From start to finish, students are under the watchful eye of the Black Hats. Incoming students are quickly inspected by a Black Hat during in-processing, with on-the-spot corrections for any discrepancies in uniform or military appearance. *Gregory Mast*

IN-PROCESSING

The 1st Battalion (Airborne), 507th Infantry, has four training companies, Alpha to Delta, committed to a continuous training cycle. During a normal training cycle, three companies will be engaged in training students, one each in the three BAC phases (ground week, tower week, and jump week). The fourth company provides additional cadre as needed, such as drop-zone coaches, and administratively prepares for the arrival of the next class of students. This off-cycle company is the fill company.

The fill company will conduct in-processing promptly at 1200 hours on the reporting date, which is the Friday prior to the start of training. Students arriving from advanced infantry training will generally arrive at 1130 by bus. All other students, either in a permanent change of station (PCS) or temporary duty (TDY) status, must arrive no later than 1200 hours of the reporting date. Late arrivals will be held over for the next class or returned to their unit of origin. Students from other services may be ordered to report to their respective detachment or liaison prior to reporting to the fill company. Do not arrive late, period. End of discussion.

In-processing covers all the administrative details necessary to check in as a student at BAC. In other words, it is a very busy afternoon, and incoming students are rarely released from duty until well after 1800 hours. Among the afternoon's events are adjutant general, finance, transportation, billeting assignment, equipment issue, platoon/squad assignment, and briefings on standards of personal conduct and military appearance.

GENERAL GUIDELINES FOR REPORTING STUDENTS

- Wear BDUs or ACUs. Jungle boots, boots with toe and heel caps (e.g., "jump boots"), or any boots with waffled or rippled soles are not authorized for wear at BAC. Boots should be clean and free of dirt. Black leather boots should be highly polished.

- Students must meet all uniform and grooming standards outlined in Army Regulation 670-1.

- Arrive with a minimum of ten copies of orders, or Department of the Army (DA) Form 1610 with fund site, which assigns or attaches you to the 1/507th Infantry for airborne training. Students from other services may be required to bring fifteen copies of their orders.

- BAC volunteers may not attend the course in a leave, permissive TDY, or permissive jump status.

- Students reporting to the BAC in a permanent change of station (PCS) or temporary duty (TDY) en-route status must have their health and dental records, finance records, and Field 201 File in their possession.

- Students older than the age of thirty-five must have their EKG and medical age waivers.

One of the most important events is the issue of your roster number, which for all practical purposes becomes your name for the next three weeks. You will be addressed by your roster number or by the term "Airborne" during BAC. Roster numbers are applied to the front of the helmet, large black numbers on a white background. The roster number is also applied to student equipment such as canteens and ankle braces. Male students receive a three-digit number, female students a two-digit number. Officers' roster numbers will be preceded by an *A*, NCOs by an *N*, and cadets by a *C*. Officers and NCOs are expected to act in leadership positions while they are students at BAC.

If a student is recycled during training, a letter will be added to the end of the roster number to indicate this. The letter *G* indicates that the student was recycled during ground week, a *T* indicates tower week, and a *J* indicates jump week.

During jump week, students may receive additional designators applied to their helmets. Chalk leaders will be identified by *CL* on the right and left side of the helmet. A chalk is one planeload of jumpers. The letter *B* indicates the break jumper, where the stick breaks between inboard and outboard jumpers on the aircraft.

This student's roster number indicates that she (two digits) is a cadet (C). Males have three-digit roster numbers. The initials marked on the number indicate that she has just received a jumpmaster personnel inspection (JMPI). The student roster number is used for identification during BAC and is applied to helmets, canteens, and other student equipment. *Hans Halberstadt*

MEET THE BLACK HATS

"Black Hats" are the cadre, or instructional staff, at BAC. The nickname derives from the distinctive black baseball cap that they wear, and they are "The Man" during your training at BAC. They are more than instructors, because in a very tangible way they *are* the Airborne School. They are the custodians of tradition, and they are the link that joins paratroopers of the past with paratroopers of the future, with every new paratrooper that they train. It is difficult, demanding duty. Not every soldier can be a paratrooper, and not every airborne sergeant has what it takes to become a Sergeant Airborne. The cadre are highly trained at Fort Benning before they are awarded the prized black cap and must continually demonstrate proficiency in order to wear it.

Training at BAC is conducted in a highly disciplined atmosphere, and when students speak to a Black Hat they are expected to be at the position of attention or parade rest. Black Hats are addressed as "sergeant airborne," or "petty officer airborne" if he or she is from the navy. They deserve your respect, and they expect to receive it. Students arriving from army basic training may be in for a shock, because drill sergeants are coddlers by comparison to Black Hats. This discipline, like everything at BAC, is driven by practical reasons. The cadre has a limited amount of time to impart information and training in the dangerous skills of military parachuting.

The cadre's main function is to teach you how to get from the aircraft to the ground without killing yourself or injuring others around you. The method of instruction has changed little since World War II. Black Hats must recite from memory, verbatim, training scripts during periods of formal instruction. Some of the scripts have been around since the late 1940s and early 1950s. During the instruction, one Black Hat will be the primary instructor, with other Black Hats acting as demonstrators. One Black Hat called this formalized method of presentation "kabuki," which is not far off the mark. The cadre rehearse these classes with the intensity of stage actors, and their delivery is intended to grab the attention of tired, sleepy students who, depending on the time of year, are either hot, sweaty, and miserable or cold, wet, and miserable.

The Black Hats demonstrate the proper methods and procedures, and students repeat them until they get it right. The training is physically demanding, with a premium placed on attention to detail.

During formal periods of instruction, Black Hats demonstrate the topic material in a highly synchronized and precise manner. These entertaining presentations are a jump school tradition that grabs the attention of tired students and is an effective training aid. *Gregory Mast*

Black Hats critique student performance quickly, bluntly, and with no sugar coating. For some students this will be the first time in their lives that they have received an honest assessment of their performance, not padded to protect their self-esteem. *Gregory Mast*

A Black Hat delivers a class at the base of the thirty-four-foot tower. A paratrooper who attended jump school in the 1950s would find the instruction familiar, because many of the training scripts have changed little since that time. Black Hats recite the scripts verbatim, ensuring uniformity of training. *Gregory Mast*

A Black Hat keeps score during performance-oriented training. Students are rated as "go" or "no go" based on their performance. A "no go" rating will cause a student to be recycled or dropped from the course. *Gregory Mast*

BECOMING A BLACK HAT

"When I came back to the Basic Airborne Course in 1990, it was impressed upon me that the standards of the school were kept at a very high level, and nobody gets to wear a black hat without demonstrating a very good knowledge of a block of subject matter and the ability to teach that material in a highly professional way. You have to memorize a lot of material, practice delivering the class, and finally make a presentation to the school's sergeant major, who decides if you're good enough for the hat.

"I was told to teach the first actual block of practical instruction students receive, 'mock door.' It took me several weeks to learn how to teach this material, and the other instructors were constantly making sure I was either teaching the class or studying the material. I carried the script around in the cargo pocket of my BDU pants, and if there wasn't anything else happening, I was required to be memorizing this script. 'Sing, rag hat!' the Black Hats would say if you weren't working on the material, since apprentice instructors wore the maroon airborne beret.

"Presenting the material is called 'singing the class,' and when your platoon sergeant and other supervisors think you are ready, you sing for the sergeant major. All the other instructors are present, but only the sergeant major decides if you get the hat or not. I got mine on the first try, after about six weeks of study."

—1st Sgt. Ed Howard, USA (Ret.)

Black Hats are experienced military professionals. The hardware on this Black Hat's uniform indicates that he is a combat veteran (combat infantryman badge), a master parachutist (star and wreath on top of the jump wings), and has participated in one combat jump (the service star on the badge). He and others like him create the future of the airborne with each new paratrooper they train. *Hans Halberstadt*

Black Hats have a multitude of responsibilities, in addition to student instruction. Here a member of the cadre is acting as the drop zone safety officer (DZSO) at Fryar Drop Zone during student jump operations. *Gregory Mast*

Black Hat assignments are not gender restricted. Female Black Hats meet the same standards as their male counterparts, and each training company has at least one female instructor. *Hans Halberstadt*

A Black Hat administers the Army Physical Fitness Test during day one of BAC. Students who fail the APFT are deemed not to be physically qualified for airborne training and are returned to their units. *Gregory Mast*

Camaraderie and strong sense of esprit de corps among paratroopers is one goal of airborne training. Black Hats are more than just instructors. They also act as mentors, coaches, and role models for the students. The never-ending training cycle is relentless, but most Black Hats manage to maintain a sense of humor through it all. *Gregory Mast*

This Black Hat is a chief petty officer (E-7) in the navy. That Black Hats come from all four major U.S. military services is a reflection of the fact that Fort Benning is the primary source of basic parachute training for the U.S armed forces. *Gregory Mast*

The Black Hats give the students all the information, training, and assistance needed to pass the course, if the student chooses to pay attention and learn. Quick learners are rewarded with less time in the harness. Slow learners are penalized with more repetitions until they get it right, and the stupid are sent back to their home units.

This brings us to the cadre's secondary function, which is to weed out the physically weak and those students who pose a risk to others. The harsh reality of life is that there is more to being a paratrooper than just riding a parachute to the ground. Soldiers who injure themselves or others due to their own physical weakness or carelessness are liabilities to their units. Airborne operations are high risk and require a higher standard of fitness and training than standard army operations. Students will be given every opportunity to pass the course, even what some might consider special assistance. However, those who cannot keep up with physical training or cannot learn to properly execute jump procedures will be dropped from the course, for their own safety and for the safety of their comrades.

Black Hats come from the four major services because students come from all U.S. services, as well as from foreign services. This is unusual for an army school and is a reflection of the diverse composition of the student body. Black Hats are experienced military professionals and experts in their respective fields. Many are now combat veterans, and it is not unusual to find a Black Hat with multiple combat tours.

As more than one Black Hat pointed out, any heavy object can make a static-line jump. Gravity does all the hard work. This does not minimize the actions that a paratrooper takes while under a deployed canopy, but speaks to the fact that what happens before, during, and after the jump is what makes the distinction between being a paratrooper or merely air-delivered cargo. The Black Hats create that difference with every new paratrooper that they train.

THREE

All periods of formal instruction are conducted outside, regardless of weather. Some bleachers are covered, some are not, but all are hot during the summer and cold during the winter. *Gregory Mast*

Ground Week: Hook Up

Students listen to a briefing prior to the start of the two-mile run. Male students must complete the run in 15:54 or better, while female students must finish in 18:54 or better. *Hans Halberstadt*

OVERVIEW

The three weeks of BAC are divided into two phases. The first and second weeks form the ground and tower training phase and are called "ground week" and "tower week" respectively. Week three forms the jump training phase and is called "jump week." Each week has specific learning objectives that must be mastered before a student is allowed to move on to the next week or phase. Instructional methods at BAC generally begin with a conference demonstration given by the instructors, followed by practical application exercises that are repeated until a student demonstrates proficiency. These are time-tested methods, developed and evolved from more than sixty years' experience at Fort Benning.

Prior to becoming a Black Hat, a noncommissioned officer must successfully complete a formal program of training and evaluation, called the "India Program." NCOs in the India Program provide assistance and support to the training companies, such as augmenting the Black Hats during the administration of the APFT on the first day of jump school. *Hans Halberstadt*

A student demonstrates the correct position for the flexed-arm hang test. For some students, jump school lasts less than ten seconds, the minimum required to pass this test. *Hans Halberstadt*

There are no academics at BAC, no course work, and no formal classroom sessions. Students are expected to watch, learn, and do, mastering the skills through rote and repetition. There is a reason behind this method. Actions that may save a paratrooper's life must become instinctual, performed without thinking or trying to remember which textbook solution to apply. If a student has a parachute malfunction, there is very little time to execute corrective actions. That is why students are drilled over and over and over on procedures, until the procedures become second nature and can be performed without conscious thought.

The Basic Airborne Course program of instruction identifies five learning objectives that students must master during ground week. Students will also learn basic safety concepts, such as the five points of performance, explained following. Each day of ground week begins with physical training (PT), with the APFT administered on the first day of training. The learning objectives, to be discussed in more detail later, are to:

- Don and adjust the main and reserve parachutes

- Identify components inside a C-130 and C-17 aircraft and respond to actions inside the aircraft using the mock door

- Exit the thirty-four-foot tower

- Execute parachute landing falls off the lateral drift apparatus

- Perform methods of recovery

Army Field Manual FM 3-21.220, *Static Line Parachuting Techniques and Training,* is the authoritative source document for training operations at BAC and tactical airborne operations in the U.S. Army. Specific techniques and commands included in this book have been taken from this manual.

BAC ENTRANCE EXAM, DAY ONE

The first day of jump school starts before dawn, under the harsh orange glow of sodium lights. By time the sun has risen, the class will be 10 to 15 percent smaller, leaving behind the students who failed to meet the BAC entrance standards. This first major event is a two-part test of physical ability, the flexed-arm hang test and the Army Physical Fitness Test. This is evaluated like everything else at BAC, as a "go" or "no go." Students either pass or fail on evaluated events. There are no grey areas. Students who fail may be recycled to the next class or dropped from the program, depending on the decision of the cadre.

FLEXED-ARM HANG TEST

The purpose of the flexed-arm hang test is to determine if the student has adequate upper-body strength to control his or her canopy during descent. The T10 canopy used by students is steered by "slipping" the suspension risers, which requires strength and endurance to execute correctly and safely. In this test the student must execute one chin-up and hold that position for at least ten seconds. Female students typically have more difficulty with this requirement than their male counterparts, as there are not separate standards by gender. The specific standards are outlined following:

- The student must grasp the bar with thumbs around the bar and palms facing toward the body.

- The student raises his/her body (with no assistance) until the chin is over the bar and the arms are flexed at the elbow: in other words, executing one chin-up. Feet must be free of the ground.

- The timer will start the stopwatch as soon as the student assumes the flexed-arm position. The student holds the position as long as possible.

- Performance of the test is terminated if the chin touches the bar, tilts backward or upward, or moves below the horizontal bar.

- Legs and trunk should remain motionless throughout the entire test. Knees must not be raised, and kicking is not permitted.

- The score is the number of seconds (rounded up to the nearest second) the student holds the hanging position, in one test only. The student must maintain the flexed-arm position for at least ten seconds, after which the student will be instructed to terminate the test.

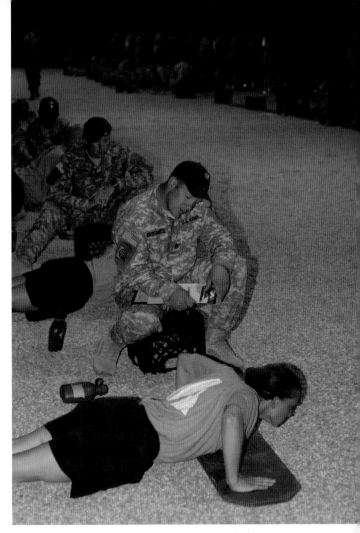

Pushups begin! The minimum required is forty-two for men and nineteen for women. Black Hats keep a close count on all repetitions, ensuring they are correct and complete. *Hans Halberstadt*

Students wait their turn at the position of parade rest during the APFT. The training at BAC is conducted in an atmosphere of high discipline. *Hans Halberstadt*

Students who arrive in good physical shape will find the APFT to be a piece of cake. Physical training for BAC should emphasize running, with the goal of being able to complete a five-mile run in forty-five minutes. *Hans Halberstadt*

This Black Hat, a navy petty officer, surveys the incoming class as they prepare for the timed two-mile run, the final event in the APFT. Every four weeks the Black Hats get a new class of students. The Black Hats jokingly call this endless training "Ground Hog Day," in reference to the movie of that name in which the same day is repeated over and over. The average Black Hat will train nearly five thousand new paratroopers during his or her assignment at Fort Benning. *Hans Halberstadt*

The battalion S-3, or operations officer, is responsible for the training operations of BAC. His shop schedules and coordinates all the assets necessary to conduct the training and provides supervision of these activities. Here the S-3 noncommissioned officer in charge (NCOIC) acts as the timekeeper for the two-mile run. *Hans Halberstadt*

ARMY PHYSICAL FITNESS TEST (APFT)

Students who successfully complete the flexed-arm hang test will take the Army Physical Fitness Test (APFT), which consists of pushups, sit-ups, and a timed two-mile run. In order to pass, all students, regardless of age, must score at least 180 points, or 60 points in each event using the 17 to 21-year age group scale. Students must pass each individual event before taking the next event, starting with pushups, then sit-ups, then the two-mile run. The test is administered by the guidelines established in Army Field Manual FM 21-20, *Physical Fitness Training*.

Male students must complete at least forty-two correct pushups within two minutes in order to pass. Female students must complete nineteen correct pushups. Students who pass this event remain with their stick, while those who fail are isolated and given a remedial test. If they pass the remedial, they may continue on to the next event. If not, they are recycled to the next class or dropped from the course.

In the second event, male and female students must complete at least fifty-three correct sit-ups in a two-minute period. The same procedure followed in the pushups test applies to students who fail this event. Students who pass will proceed to the two-mile run.

The two-mile run is conducted on a flat track that circles the tower training area. Male students must complete the run in 15:54 or better in order to pass. Female students have to complete the run in 18:54 seconds or better in order to pass. Students who fail the run will be recycled to the next class or dropped from the course.

Students who pass will then double-time back to the barracks for a quick shower. Then they will double-time back to the tower area for a demonstration of the basic concepts of military parachuting, which they will have to master over the next three weeks.

AIRBORNE ORIENTATION, DAY ONE

The first afternoon of BAC is largely occupied by a group demonstration given by the cadre to the students. The orientation takes place near the Airborne Walk at Eubanks Field, not far from where the APFT was administered to the class earlier in the day. The purpose of the demonstration is to inform the students about the training they can expect during ground week and tower week. The Black Hats demonstrate how each action is correctly executed, as well as how it is incorrectly executed.

One primary instructor and at least seventeen demonstrators will acquaint the class with the mock door, the thirty-four-foot mock tower, the lateral drift apparatus, suspended harness, swing-landing trainer, and 250-foot free tower. The Black Hats will demonstrate parachute landing falls (PLFs) and door exit procedures.

WELCOME TO THE BASIC AIRBORNE COURSE!

"I went to the Basic Airborne Course in 1966. The first day, right after we finished the PT test, they assembled the whole class in the bleachers for a parachuting demonstration by the Golden Knights, the army's parachute team. One of the instructors narrated the demonstration while reading from a prepared script that named each of the jumpers and the number of their jumps.

" 'Welcome to the Basic Airborne Course,' he said. "Above me now is Sgt. Bob Smith, with 450 jumps, and Sgt. Fred Brown with 390 jumps," and so forth, as they deployed their parachutes.

"This narrator couldn't see what was actually happening behind him-one of the jumpers had a major malfunction. His canopy was all balled up, and he was falling toward the ground at high velocity long after the other jumpers had opened their chutes. The narrator was oblivious to all this, but we could see something was not quite right.

"Finally, at about the height of the tops of the 250-foot towers, I noticed this jumper finally deploy his reserve. It caught a little air, but not much, before he hit the ground. I remember him bouncing what seemed like about ten feet into the air. The narrator continued reading from his script as if this demonstration was entirely normal and according to plan.

"The ambulances arrived, and the medics began to scrape up the residue of this poor guy while the narrator on the PA system continued to read his script, extolling the virtues of the airborne and the Basic Airborne Course. I don't think the guy could possibly have survived, and, all in all, the demonstration failed to motivate the class to become super-duper paratroopers. The next morning, I think the class was missing about one hundred students."

—Col. Gerald Schumacher, U.S. Army Special Forces (Ret.)

PT SCHEDULE, GROUND WEEK

Every training day during ground week and tower week begins with a period of formal physical training. Students are evaluated on their performance. Failure to complete any portion of the assigned PT satisfactorily or dropping out of any formation run may result in the student's ejection from the course. This is the stated policy. Some exceptions may be made, but they are rare.

Day two of ground week consists of guerilla drills and grass drills. According to Army Field Manual FM 21-20, *Physical Fitness Training,* guerrilla exercises combine individual and partner exercises, which can be used to improve agility, cardiorespiratory (CR) endurance, muscular endurance, and to some degree muscular strength. These drills require soldiers to change their positions quickly and perform various basic skills while moving forward. Grass drills are exercise movements that feature rapid changes in body position. These are vigorous drills, which, when properly done, exercise all the major muscle groups. Soldiers should respond to commands as fast as possible and do all movements at top speed. They continue to do multiple repetitions of each exercise until the next command is given.

Day three is a 3.2-mile formation run. All runs at BAC are conducted at a pace of nine minutes per mile, plus or minus fifteen seconds. Students cannot fall more than two steps behind their original place in the formation. Failure to complete the runs more than twice is cause for dismissal from airborne training. Male and female students run in the same formation, and there are not separate standards for this event.

Day four is a return to guerilla/grass drills. Day five is a four-mile formation run.

The finish line is the real start of jump school for those students who pass the APFT. The man in white shorts was the first student from the newly formed Iraqi army to attend BAC. *Gregory Mast*

Every training day in ground and tower week starts with an organized PT session. Physical training starts well before dawn so that the cadre can take maximum advantage of the daylight hours for parachute training. *Gregory Mast*

Sit-ups are the second event in the Army Physical Fitness Test. The minimum standard is the same for male and female airborne students: fifty-three complete and correct sit-ups in two minutes. Standards for all exercises in the APFT are established in Army Field Manual 21-20, "Physical Fitness Training." *Gregory Mast*

Students who fail either pushups or sit-ups are given a re-test, after being segregated from the class. If they pass the re-test, they will rejoin the APFT in progress. If they fail the re-test, they will either be returned to their unit of origin or recycled to the next class, depending upon the decision of the training cadre. *Gregory Mast*

Students who arrive at BAC physically unprepared do not last long. This student barely made it past sunrise on the first day of jump school. Students are solely responsible for their physical condition, and no excuses are accepted for poor preparation. *Gregory Mast*

(Above) The T10D parachute, currently in use as the standard parachute for mass tactical drops, is a direct descendent of the parachute that carried paratroopers into Normandy on D-day. The T10 has been in use since the 1950s, with modifications. The U.S. Army is developing a replacement for the aging T10 series, the advanced tactical parachute system (ATPS), which is expected to be in service by 2010. *Gregory Mast*

(Left) On the first day of jump school, students are briefed on the training they will undergo over the next three weeks. This briefing is called airborne orientation, or airborne 5000. A platoon of instructors demonstrate every piece of equipment used during training, while one Black Hat provides a narration, explaining in succinct detail the purpose of every apparatus, exercise, and drill used to prepare the students to jump out of "perfectly good" airplanes. *Gregory Mast*

THE T10 PARACHUTE: YOUR BEST FRIEND

The standard parachute, and its component parts, that the U.S. Army uses for training and operations is a direct descendent of the parachute used in World War II. Although the current version, the T10D, embodies many refinements, it remains largely unchanged from the parachutes that delivered paratroopers to Normandy on D-day. The first major learning objective for students is to master how to correctly don and adjust the main and reserve parachutes.

The student's main parachute is the T10 parachute, which, with modifications and refinements, has been in use since the 1950s. The T10 parachute assembly consists of five components: pack tray, troop harness, deployment bag, riser, and canopy. The nylon canopy, deployed using a 15- or 20-foot universal static line (USL), is a parabolic shape. It has a nominal diameter of 35 feet at its widest, measured 3 feet up from the skirt, and a diameter of 24.5 feet at the skirt. A total of thirty suspension lines connect the canopy to the riser assembly. A mesh anti-inversion net runs around the base of the canopy, which is intended to reduce certain canopy malfunctions. The anti-inversion net is sewn 18 inches down on each suspension line and is made of three 3/4-inch-square mesh of knotless, braided nylon. Depending on the jumper's total weight and relative air density, the average rates of descent are 19 to 23 feet per second. The canopies are repacked every 120 days and are suitable for airdropping personnel from as high as ten thousand feet above mean sea level (MSL).

The T10's long service life is nearing its end. Although the T10 system has served reliably for mass tactical jumps for half a century, jump injuries are on the rise, because modern soldiers are larger and carry more equipment than their predecessors. Designed to accommodate a gross tactical weight of 250 pounds, modern paratroopers can easily weigh in excess of 300 pounds when exiting the aircraft in full combat kit. An advanced tactical parachute system is under development and may be adopted to replace the T10 system before 2008.

The student's reserve parachute is the modified improved reserve parachute system (MIRPS). It is a chest-mounted emergency parachute to be used in the event that the main parachute malfunctions. It is manually activated by a ripcord and has a twenty-four-foot canopy. The MIRPS is being replaced by the soft-loop center-pull (SLCP) for reasons of safety. The SLCP can be activated easily with either hand, and the mechanism is less likely to bind when the ripcord is pulled. Students will be trained on both types of reserve parachutes while at BAC until the MIRPS is phased out.

Donning and adjusting the troop parachute harness is best done using the buddy system. This provides the best combination of speed and accuracy for parachutists to adjust and check each other's parachutes. Proper adjustment of the harness is a critical first step, not only for the comfort of the parachutist during transport but also to minimize the risk of injury during opening shock.

- The parachutist lays the assembly out with the pack tray face down and activates the waistband quick-release and releases the leg straps and the chest strap. He then checks for appropriate size and, if necessary, adjusts the size of the harness.

- The parachutist (number 1) bends slightly forward at the waist to don the parachute. A second parachutist (number 2) holds the parachute assembly by the main lift web under the canopy-release assemblies and places it on the back of number 1.

- Number 1 remains bent forward at the waist; number 2 pushes the pack tray high on number 1's back and pulls the saddle well down over the buttocks. As the adjustment is being made, number 1 fastens the chest strap and ensures that the activating lever is closed over the ball detent.

- Number 2 calls out "Left leg strap," grasps the leg strap by the quick-fit V-ring with one hand, and feels the length of the leg strap, removing any twists and turns, and hands the left leg strap to the jumper. Number 1 inserts the left leg strap through the kit bag carrying handle and snaps the quick-fit V-ring into the left ejector snap. The right leg strap is passed over the other end of the kit bag (securing it in place), and the quick-fit V-ring is snapped into the right ejector snap. The parachutist ensures that both the left and right activating levers are closed over the ball detents.

- Number 1 stands erect and checks to ensure the canopy-release assemblies are in the pockets of the shoulders.

- Number 2 locates the free-running ends of the horizontal back strap and tightens the harness until number 1 indicates it fits snugly and comfortably. The horizontal back strap is the main point of adjustment for the harness. After final adjustment, number 1 should be able to stand fully erect without straining.

- Number 1 and number 2 then change positions and repeat the previous.

- When both parachutists have donned their parachute harnesses, they face each other and make a visual inspection. They correct any discrepancies before securing the reserve parachute. All excess webbing is stowed in webbing retainers.

- The parachutist attaches the reserve parachute by cradling the parachute in his left arm with the connector snaps up and the ripcord grip in the palm of the left hand. Using the right hand, start at the pack tray and run out the waistband to remove any twists or turns.

- Thread the waistband through the two reserve waistband retainers and fasten the right connector snap to the right D-ring. Insert the safety wire in the right connector snap and then bend the wire down to safety it. Then connect the left connector snap to the left D-ring.

- Parachutists help each other in securing the waistband and forming the quick-release. They ensure that all slack is pulled out of the waistband, and the slack in the quick-release loop is about the width of two to three fingers.

THE FIVE POINTS OF PERFORMANCE

Students learn the five points of performance on their first day of training at BAC, and these are considered essential on every jump the student makes, in school and later on in the "real" world. Before each airborne operation, a jumpmaster runs through the sustained airborne training script (discussed at length in a later section). While the script is being recited, paratroopers perform the actions. The five points of performance are specific actions the parachutist performs between the time of exit from the aircraft and the recovery after landing. One or more of these points of performance are stressed with each training exercise at BAC.

The first point of performance is, "Proper exit, check body position, and count." Here, the eyes are open, the chin is on the chest, elbows are tight into the sides, and the hands are over the ends of the reserve parachute with fingers spread. The body is bent slightly forward at the waist, with the feet and knees together and knees locked to the rear. This body position ensures the jumper does not tumble on leaving the aircraft and ensures the parachute deploys correctly. On exiting the aircraft, the jumper executes a slow count of "one thousand, two thousand, three thousand, four thousand." If he feels no opening shock, the sudden deceleration caused by the opening of the canopy, he immediately activates the reserve parachute.

The second point of performance is, "Check canopy and immediately gain canopy control." To gain canopy control of the T10D parachute, the jumper reaches up and secures all four risers and simultaneously makes a 360-degree check of the canopy.

The third point of performance is, "Keep a sharp lookout for all jumpers during your entire descent." Remember the three rules of the air:

• Always look before you turn.

• Always turn right to avoid collisions.

• The lower jumper has the right of way.

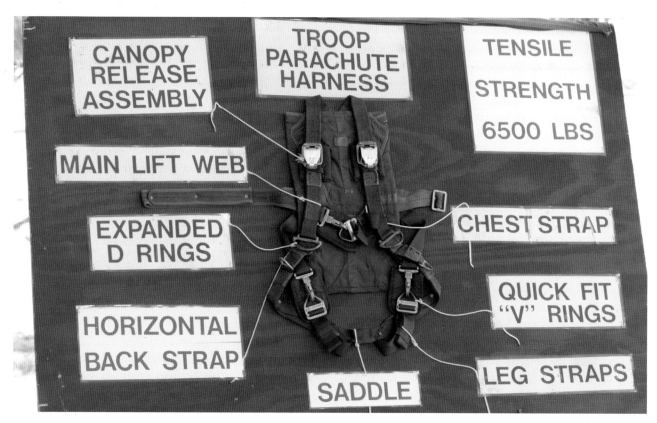

The troop parachute harness is illustrated in this training aid. Take note of the expanded D-rings, as they are referenced throughout the text. The reserve parachute is attached to the D-rings, and they provide the suspension points for the quick-release harness used when jumping with combat equipment. *Gregory Mast*

Avoid all jumpers all the way to the ground. Maintain at least a fifty-foot separation. At the end of your third point of performance, release all appropriate equipment tie-downs.

The fourth point of performance is, "Slip or turn into the wind and prepare to land." At approximately two hundred feet above ground level, the paratrooper performs a check below, and then lowers the equipment.

When jumping with a T10D parachute, the slip into the wind is performed at approximately one hundred feet above ground level. If the wind is blowing from left to right, the jumper reaches up high on the left risers and pulls them down into his chest, holding them until landing. If the wind is blowing from the rear to the front, the jumper will reach up high on his rear risers and pull them down into his chest and hold them until he lands. If the wind is blowing from the jumper's front, he pulls the front risers down into his chest and holds them until landing.

After the jumper has slipped or turned into the wind, he assumes a prepare-to-land attitude by keeping the feet and knees together, knees slightly bent, elbows tight into the sides, chin on the chest, and eyes open.

The fifth point of performance is, "Land." A parachute-landing fall is made by hitting all five points of contact: balls of feet, calf, thigh, buttocks, and the pull-up muscle. The jumper activates one of the canopy-release assemblies while remaining on the ground to prevent being dragged across the ground by the parachute. Then, the jumper remains on his back to get out of the parachute harness before placing his weapon into operation and rising to retrieve his parachute.

MOCK-DOOR TRAINING
AND ACTIONS INSIDE THE AIRCRAFT

Mock doors are basic replicas of aircraft troop doors and interior troop spaces. They are designed and used to familiarize jumpers with jump procedures and the location of standard equipment within the aircraft. In mock-door training during ground week, students learn the location of the aircraft's right and left doors and the location of the static-line hook anchor-line cables. They also learn how to properly form a bight in the static line, how to assume the shuffle and standby positions, and how to exit the aircraft mock-up. Upon exit, students rehearse the first and second points of performance, "Proper exit, check body position, and count," and "Check canopy and immediately gain canopy control." Students learn both the concept of prop blast and the actions for door-exit procedures.

Students learn the buddy method for donning and adjusting the T10 parachute and reserve. This method is not only time efficient but provides an additional safety check that all equipment is properly adjusted and connected. Multiple layers of safety checks help reduce human error, the leading cause of parachute mishaps. *Gregory Mast*

A correctly adjusted harness is very important, as some students will learn by painful lesson on the thirty-four-foot tower, swing landing trainer, or over the drop zone. During opening shock-the rapid deceleration experienced by parachutists when the canopy opens-a harness that is too loosely adjusted may slip and cause crush injuries or other trauma to the jumper. *Gregory Mast*

The heat and humidity of a summer at Fort Benning can pose a serious hazard even to those soldiers who are acclimated to these conditions. One way to keep students cool is to march them under open showers, drenching them with cold water. *Gregory Mast*

A Black Hat observes a student during mock door training, prior to exiting the thirty-four-foot tower during ground week. The mock door simulates the interior and troop door of cargo aircraft and is used to familiarize students with the location and nomenclature of equipment, rehearse actions inside the aircraft, and practice exit procedures. Mock door training, in one form or another, will be a recurring exercise throughout a paratrooper's jump career. *Gregory Mast*

The jumpmaster controls actions inside the aircraft through a standardized series of jump commands. This series of commands is so ingrained into a paratrooper's memory that veterans can repeat it, in correct order, decades after they've forgotten everything else about the army. Each command calls for specific action on the part of each parachutist. The final two commands, "Stand by" and "Go," are used for students when practicing exits from mock door trainers during ground week. Students wear a modified parachute harness with main and reserve parachute for mock-door training during ground week.

Students are coached and evaluated on these fundamental skills from the relative safety of a platform two feet above ground level. Through repetition during ground week, students learn how to safely move in an aircraft in flight, how to handle their static line, and how to make a vigorous exit from the airplane.

(Top to bottom:)

Students rehearse the first and second points of performance in mock door training during ground week. Here, a student demonstrates the first point of performance: "Proper exit, check body position, and count." After a vigorous exit, the jumper tucks his chin to his chest, holds the side of his reserve with fingers spread and elbows tucked, bends at the waist while keeping feet and knees together, and shouts his four thousand count. *Gregory Mast*

During mock door training, a student demonstrates the second point of performance: "Check canopy and immediately gain canopy control." After opening shock, the jumper examines the canopy for holes, tears, blown panels, broken suspension lines, and other damage while grasping the risers to establish canopy control. *Gregory Mast*

Students are rehearsing actions inside the aircraft during ground week mock door training. Students respond to the last two jump commands, "Stand by" and "Go," learn the "airborne shuffle" for moving safely prior to exiting, practice static-line control, and demonstrate exit procedures. *Gregory Mast*

A student demonstrates a vigorous exit during ground week mock door training. A strong exit reduces the possibility of parachute malfunctions or injury due to striking the side of the aircraft. *Gregory Mast*

THE THIRTY-FOUR-FOOT TOWER

Thirty-four feet doesn't sound that high until you are standing in the tower door and trying not to look down at the ground. During ground week, students will be introduced to the training device that will play a more prominent role in tower week. There are two sets of thirty-four-foot towers, one located at Ground Branch, located off Sightseeing Road, and the other, appropriately enough, at Tower Branch at Eubanks Field. Sitting thirty-four feet above the ground is a mock aircraft door and interior, connected to the ground by a cable and trolley system that allows students to practice exit technique, experience opening shock, and overcome fear of heights. For some students, the thirty-four-foot tower is an amusement park ride; for others, there is nothing amusing about the experience. Once a student overcomes his or her fear of heights, the worst part of the thirty-four-foot tower is trudging up the stairs, especially during tower week with combat gear.

One of the thirty-four-foot towers at Ground Branch. Once the student has overcome the fear of heights and dread of opening shock, the worst part becomes the long climb up the stairs. *Gregory Mast*

During the first week, tower training will consist of individual exits, stressing proper body position during exit and body control until opening shock. Opening shock teaches students, in a very practical way, about the value of a properly adjusted troop parachute harness. Particularly for the male students, poorly adjusted harnesses can result in injuries that are both painful and embarrassing. Male students who want to leave BAC with everything they brought with them should double- and triple-check their harness fit.

The goal of the training is to teach students the correct methods of donning and adjusting a troop parachute harness, hook-up procedures, how to execute the shuffling technique, the standby position, and how to execute the first three points of performance.

Prior to exiting the thirty-four-foot towers, both during ground and tower weeks, students rehearse their actions at a mock-door trainer located next to the tower. During the training, students are in three rotating groups. One group observes, one group trains, and the third group provides safety-support and equipment-retrieval duties. The students who are "jumping" don the parachute harness and reserve parachute and fall into line in the stairwell leading up to the top of the tower. Once inside the mock aircraft, the student's harness is connected to the trolley mechanism that will slide him down the cable after exiting the door. During individual exits, the student assumes the standby position at the door, and on the command "Go" makes a vigorous exit from the tower door.

After exit, the student executes the first three points of performance and will be evaluated on them:

- Proper exit, check body position, and count: students shout the four thousand count as they exit the mock door, while maintaining a correct tucked body position, following a strong exit.

- Check canopy and immediately gain canopy control: while descending the cable toward the mound, the student will grab the risers and perform a canopy check.

- Keep a sharp lookout for all jumpers during your entire descent: as the student approaches the mound, he will scan the ground below, simulating the procedure for checking the jumpers around him.

After a few rides down the cable, most students manage to hold a good, tight body position during opening shock. *Gregory Mast*

First exits from the thirty-four-foot tower are usually tentative and rarely executed correctly. This student is making a reluctant and weak exit, while looking at the ground instead of the horizon. Hand position on the reserve is also incorrect. *Gregory Mast*

A student makes a vigorous exit from the thirty-four-foot tower during ground week. He has his eyes on the horizon and takes a big step out of the door. *Gregory Mast*

The thirty-four-foot tower introduces students to the concept of opening shock in an eye-opening way. Students with an incorrectly adjusted troop parachute harness are in for a painful surprise. *Gregory Mast*

A student is on the lateral drift apparatus (LDA), the major components of which are visible in this photograph. The student mounts the platform and grasps the trolley. On command, a second student pulls the trolley in order to develop speed. The student on the trolley will release his grip and drop to the ground to practice parachute landing falls (PLFs). *Gregory Mast*

PARACHUTE LANDING FALLS: A CONTROLLED CRASH

The stated rate of descent for a T10 parachute is between nineteen and twenty-three feet per second, depending on the circumstances. Your mileage may vary. In plain English, this means the ground is coming up pretty fast. In order to absorb and dissipate this impact, roughly equivalent to jumping off a twelve-foot platform, the parachutist executes a parachute landing fall (PLF) upon landing. Even with a PLF, landings can be bone jarring. The majority of all jump injuries occur on landing, which is why PLFs are a part of basic, advanced, and refresher airborne training. Students will perform hundreds of PLFs while at BAC, with on-the-spot critique and evaluation provided by Black Hats.

There are three types of PLFs, dictated by the direction of wind drift on landing: 1) side, 2) front, and 3) rear. As the balls of his feet strike the ground, the parachutist begins several actions at the same time. The jumper lowers his or her chin to the chest and tenses the neck muscles. Then he brings his hands up in front of his head, with elbows in front of his chest, continuing to grasp the risers. Then he bends and twists his torso sharply in the opposite direction of the fall, forcing the body into an arc. The twisting motion of the hips pushes both knees in the direction of the fall, exposing the second through the fifth points of contact (calf, thigh, buttock, and side of the back). As the PLF is completed in the direction of drift, the parachutist maintains the tension in his neck to prevent his head from striking the ground. After completing the PLF, the jumper activates one canopy-release assembly to keep from being dragged.

During ground week, PLF training is conducted from a two-foot platform, a four-foot platform, and from the lateral drift apparatus. The lateral drift apparatus is a trolley device that simulates the motion of a descending canopy and creates a more realistic training environment for students to practice PLFs, from all directions: side, front, and rear. The student grasps the handles of the trolley and is pulled along the cable by another student. On command, while the trolley is moving, the student will release the handles and drop to the ground, executing a PLF upon impact. Even though the landing surface is "soft" (all things are relative at BAC), students find this training to be bruising and quickly learn how to do a proper PLF. The height of the drop depends upon the height of the student. Shorter students have a longer drop. (Hey, no one ever said life is fair.)

A student double-times back to the thirty-four-foot tower to receive an evaluation of his performance from the Black Hats. *Gregory Mast*

Eyes on the horizon, a student prepares to exit the thirty-four-foot tower during ground week. Students will spend two days conducting tower training that week. *Gregory Mast*

Illustration of parachute landing falls (PLF) sequence from FM 3-21.220, *Static Line Parachuting Techniques and Training*. The parachutist distributes the shock of landing by rolling and making five points of contact (the balls of the feet, calf, thigh, buttock, and pull-up muscles).

A student is at the start of a PLF sequence after dropping from the lateral drift apparatus. The Black Hats observe student performance intently and will make the student repeat the exercise until he performs it correctly. *Gregory Mast*

METHODS OF RECOVERY: LANDING CAN BE A DRAG

Even a slight breeze on the drop zone can pose a danger to parachutists. One very real danger is the risk of being dragged behind your canopy after landing. This risk is minimized by activating the canopy-release assembly immediately after completing the parachute landing fall. However, a jumper might find himself being dragged before he can complete the task. Students are taught to deal with this situation, as well as how to correctly stow their air items, during methods of recovery training.

Canopy-release assemblies, sometimes referred to as "capewells," are quick-release mechanisms that connect the suspension risers to the parachute harness. Before the canopy-release assemblies can be activated, the safety clip must be pulled down to expose the cable loop. There are two ways to activate the canopy-release assembly. One is the hand-to-shoulder method, and the other is the hand-assist method. The cable-loop release does not require a great deal of strength to activate, and, if the parachutist is injured, he can easily activate it by the thumb or fingers of either hand.

Students are taught to activate the canopy-release assemblies by using the hand-towed drag pad. One student, in parachute harness, lies on his back while attached to the pad, and is dragged across the ground by two other students. This allows the student to practice activating the assemblies under stress, while giving the draggers a cardio workout.

During this training, students also learn how to remove their harness and reserve parachute while on their backs. They are then taught to engage their weapon, if they have one, and rise on one knee to retrieve their parachute.

A student is preparing to drop from the lateral drift apparatus. The trolley's four handles allow students to practice PLFs from the front, rear, and both sides. *Hans Halberstadt*

A student leaves the platform of the lateral drift apparatus. The class is arranged so that students waiting their turn can observe the other students' performance. *Gregory Mast*

The student is at the end of a PLF sequence after dropping from the lateral drift apparatus. The landing surface is gravel and by the standards of BAC considered to be "soft." The height of the drop depends on the height of the student, with shorter students having a longer fall than their taller classmates. *Gregory Mast*

Students learn by observing the mistakes of other students. Occasionally, a student screw-up will momentarily silence the onlookers. A noisy camaraderie develops over the three weeks of BAC, and the students will offer their unsolicited performance evaluations. *Gregory Mast*

GROUND WEEK SUMMARY

One down, two to go. Some students will not get past ground week, either due to injury or PT failure. All students will be slightly banged up from the week's activities, but generally most students will be looking forward to a weekend's liberty. During nonduty hours, students are normally free to travel within a fifty-mile radius of Fort Benning, Georgia, without a valid leave form. Travel outside the radius requires an authorization from the company commander. You must return well rested and on time for company-designated formations and training. Basic Airborne Course students are not authorized to consume alcoholic beverages within twenty-four hours prior to a training day and are not authorized to possess alcoholic beverages in the billets. Students who violate provisions of the Uniform Code of Military Justice (UCMJ) will be quickly disciplined and may be permanently dropped from airborne training with subsequent assignment as a nongraduate. Finally, do not even think of going to establishments that have been declared off limits. They are off limits for a reason, and getting caught patronizing these establishments will get you a one-way ticket back to your unit, with an Article 15 awarded in lieu of jump wings.

FOUR

Students are seated in stick formation inside the mock door trainer, simulating the inside of a cargo aircraft. During tower week's mock door training, the students rehearse the entire jump-command sequence and the associated actions. *Gregory Mast*

Tower Week: Check Equipment

Airborne students are on the first day of tower week. BAC is conducted in an atmosphere of military discipline, and students move in formation from place to place. *Gregory Mast*

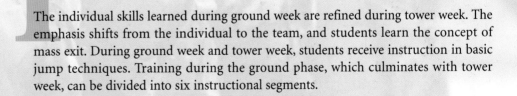

T The individual skills learned during ground week are refined during tower week. The emphasis shifts from the individual to the team, and students learn the concept of mass exit. During ground week and tower week, students receive instruction in basic jump techniques. Training during the ground phase, which culminates with tower week, can be divided into six instructional segments.

Students rehearse mass-exit procedures from the thirty-four-foot tower during tower week. During ground week, students performed individual exits. *Hans Halberstadt*

• Actions inside the aircraft: To ensure that the maximum number of parachutists can safely exit an aircraft, a means of controlling their actions inside the aircraft just before exiting is necessary. The jumpmaster maintains control by issuing jump commands. Each command calls for specific action on the part of each parachutist.

• Body control until opening shock: Due to aircraft speed and air turbulence around the rear of the aircraft, the parachutist must exit properly and maintain the correct body position after exiting. This action reduces spinning and tumbling in the air and allows for proper parachute deployment.

• Parachute control during descent: Parachute control is essential to avoid other parachutists in the air and to avoid hitting obstacles on the ground.

• Parachute landing fall execution: The PLF is a landing technique that enables the parachutist to distribute the landing shock over his entire body to reduce the impact and the possibility of injury.

• Parachute control on landing: The parachutist releases one canopy-release assembly after landing. Winds on the drop zone may cause a parachutist to be injured from being dragged along the ground.

• Physical training: This is included in each day of ground training. Students who cannot progress in daily physical training are referred to a board that decides either to recycle them or to return them to their unit. Daily exercises are designed to condition the muscle groups that play a significant part in jumping.

The training apparatuses used during tower week are the thirty-four-foot towers, the swing-landing trainer (SLT), the mock door for mass-exit training, the suspended harness, and the 250-foot free tower. The specific learning objectives for this week are:

- Respond to jump commands in the C-130 and C-17, and execute individual and mass exits using the mock door

- Demonstrate proficiency in fixed-wing aircraft exits from the thirty-four-foot tower, wearing combat equipment

- Demonstrate techniques for deploying the reserve parachute. Students will learn procedures for both modified improved reserve parachute (MIRPS) and soft-loop center-pull (SLCP).

- Control the T10 risers from the suspended harness

- Execute parachute landing falls correctly with the T10 parachute from the swing-landing trainer

- Execute a drop from the 250-foot free tower using the modified T10 canopy

PT SCHEDULE, TOWER WEEK

Physical training intensifies during tower week. As in ground week, failure to complete any portion of the assigned PT satisfactorily or dropping out of any formation run may result in the student's ejection from the course.

Days one and two include a four-mile formation run. Male and female students run in the same formation, and there are no separate standards for this event. Like all runs at BAC, they are conducted at a pace of nine minutes per mile, plus or minus fifteen seconds, and students cannot fall more than two steps behind their original place in the formation. Failure to complete a run more than twice is cause for dismissal from airborne training.

Day three consists of log drills and circuit training. Log drills, as established in FM 21-20, *Physical Fitness Training*, are team-conditioning exercises. They develop strength and muscular endurance, as well as teamwork. Log drills consist of six different exercises numbered in a set pattern. The drills are intense, and teams should complete them in fifteen minutes. The teams have six to eight students per log.

Circuit training is a group of stations or areas where students perform specific tasks or exercises for a defined period of time. Circuits are designed to increase the student's CR endurance, muscular endurance, strength, flexibility, and speed.

Day four is more log drills and circuit training. Day five includes a five-mile, off-track formation run.

Log drills have been a favored method of team building exercise by the army since before World War II. During tower week, PT includes this classic exercise.

Prior to mock door training during tower week, Black Hats conduct hit-it exercises. These exercises are part of sustained airborne training that all jumpers conduct prior to jumps, during which they rehearse actions they take after exiting the aircraft. *Gregory Mast*

After hooking up, the student forms a bight, or loop, in his static line, four inches in hand, two inches exposed below. *Gregory Mast*

OLD SCHOOL

"I went to the school in 1962, and some things have changed a lot since then. For one thing, we ran in boots and uniform pants, not running shoes and shorts as today. The surface under the 250-foot towers was gravel then, not plowed earth. All the students lived in World War II wooden barracks that were about thirty degrees warmer than the outside air, and that was hot enough in July.

"During tower week, I screwed up on one of the evolutions and was directed to take a couple of turns around the one-mile track as punishment. While running, I passed out from the heat, and when I regained consciousness found that I had been given a drop slip: they wanted to throw me out of the course.

"I was a bit brash at the time and went to see the school commander, a full colonel. 'Sir,' I told him, 'I came here to be a paratrooper!'

" 'Well, you aren't going to be one,' the colonel said, 'you've been dropped!'

" 'I don't think so!' I replied, and struck his desk with my fist, accidentally breaking his swagger stick in the process.

"This performance seemed to impress the commander, fortunately in the way I had hoped. He let me stay, and I made it through the course."

—Sgt. 1st Class Bill Knox, USA (Ret.)

ACTIONS INSIDE THE AIRCRAFT; MOCK-DOOR TRAINING

Students were introduced to the mock-door trainers during ground week, where they learned individual actions. The training during tower week builds upon those lessons and adds the concept of mass exits. The objective of a mass exit is to empty the airplane of parachutists, at one-second intervals, safely and efficiently. Students must learn to move quickly and safely within the cramped confines of an aircraft, wearing heavy gear and a constricting harness, while keeping positive control of their static line and not fouling the jumper in front or the jumper behind. Strict adherence to proper procedure is absolutely necessary during a mass exit, because the potential for mishap is great.

Students rehearse the complete sequence of jump commands during advanced mock-door training. The jumpmaster gives a sequence of jump commands to ensure positive control of parachutists inside the aircraft and immediately before exiting. Every command requires specific actions by each parachutist. There are slight variations in the commands, depending on the aircraft, and during tower week training, students learn the commands for both the Lockheed C-130 Hercules and the Boeing C-17A Globemaster III. The jumpmaster shouts commands, but, as a backup, he also uses arm-and-hand signals with each command due to aircraft noise. The jumpers repeat the commands in unison to ensure that all of them are aware of what is going on around them.

Jump commands are detailed at length in Army Field Manual FM 3-21.220, *Static Line Parachuting Techniques and Training*, and quoted liberally here. The sequence following is what is used at BAC:

"Ten minutes" is the first time warning the jumpmaster gives when the aircraft is ten minutes from the drop zone. The jumpmaster holds his hands with palms toward the jumpers with all ten fingers extended. The jumpers in the aircraft repeat this three times, first to their right, then to their left, then to the jumper in front of them: "Ten minutes, ten minutes, ten minutes."

"Get ready" is the first jump command. This command alerts the parachutists seated in the aircraft and directs their complete attention to the jumpmaster. The jumpmaster starts the command with his arms at his sides and gives the arm-and-hand signal by extending both arms to the front at shoulder level with his palms facing the parachutists. He gives the oral command "Get ready," then returns to the start position with arms at the sides.

The students have just responded to the "Sound off for equipment check" command. The first jumper in the stick indicates when the check is complete by his extended hand and shout of "All okay, jumpmaster." *Gregory Mast*

The student jumper's static line is routed over the appropriate shoulder and fastened to the top carrying handle of the reserve parachute. Parachutists do not remove the static-line snap hook from the reserve parachute after the jumpmaster personnel inspections (JMPI) or anytime before the command "Hook up."

Jumpers relay this command, in unison, toward the front of the aircraft, and then each one leans forward and places both hands on his knees. Each parachutist positions his foot nearest the jump door under the seat and places his foot nearest the pilot's compartment in the aisle.

"Outboard personnel, stand up" is the second jump command. For this command, the arm-and-hand signal has two parts. The jumpmaster starts at the shoulders, index and middle fingers extended and joined, with remaining fingers and thumbs curled to the palms. He gives the command "Outboard personnel," lowers the arms down to the sides at a 45-degree angle, and locks the elbows. The jumpmaster then gives the command "Stand up." He extends and joins the fingers and thumb of each hand, rotates the hands so the palms face up, and then raises the arms straight overhead, keeping the elbows locked.

At this command, all jumpers repeat the command toward the front of the aircraft. Then, the parachutists sitting nearest the outboard side of the aircraft stand up, raise and secure the seats, face the jump doors, and assume the shuffle position.

"Inboard personnel, stand up" is the third jump command. This arm-and-hand signal also has two parts. The jumpmaster starts with the hands centered on the chest at shoulder level, index and middle fingers extended and joined, remaining fingers and thumbs curled to the palms. He gives the command "Inboard personnel," extends the arms forward at a forty-five-degree angle toward the inboard seats, and locks the elbows. The jumpmaster then gives the command "Stand up." He first rotates his arms to the sides and down at a forty-five-degree angle. Then he extends and joins the fingers and thumb of each hand, rotates his hands so the palms face up, and raises his arms straight overhead, keeping the elbows locked.

The parachutists seated inboard react in the same manner as the outboard personnel. Once standing, they repeat the commands over the shoulder that is closest to the skin of the aircraft. Once all jumpers are standing, they merge into a single line. The first three jumpers in the stick extend and lock their arms to get proper distance.

Students are taught to repeat all jump commands prior to responding to the command. Jump aircraft are noisy, and only the first few jumpers can actually hear the jumpmaster. Jumpmasters also use standard hand and arm signals with each command. Here, the jumpmaster has just given the command "Stand by," alerting the jumpers that the next command is "Go." *Gregory Mast*

Mock door training is used to rehearse actions inside the aircraft, such as static-line handling. Here, students hand the assistant jumpmaster, known as the "safety," their static lines prior to exiting the aircraft. Actions such as this are rehearsed over and over on the ground so that they are second nature once the students are onboard a jump aircraft. The safety controls the static lines to prevent jumpers from becoming entangled on them as they exit the airplane. *Gregory Mast*

(Right) Once outside the door, students practice the first and second points of performance, just as they did during ground week. *Gregory Mast*

(Below) After the last jumper in a stick has exited the mock door, the cadre will also rehearse jumpmaster actions such as checking for a towed jumper. This is more for student familiarization with what happens on a jump aircraft than for training the Black Hats. *Gregory Mast*

The remaining jumpers in the stick move closely together until their reserve is touching the parachute pack tray in front of them.

"Hook up" is the fourth jump command. The jumpmaster begins with his arms either extended directly overhead with elbows locked or with arms bent, hands at shoulder level. He forms a hook with the index finger of each hand and forms fists with the remaining fingers and thumb of each hand. As he gives the oral command, he moves his arms down and up in a pumping motion. He repeats the arm-and-hand signal at least three times.

After repeating this command, each parachutist detaches the static-line snap hook from the top carrying handle of the reserve parachute and hooks up to the appropriate anchor-line cable, with the open portion of the snap hook toward the outboard side of the aircraft. Each parachutist must ensure that the snap hook locks properly. The safety wire is inserted in the hole and folded down. To protect the eyes, the wire is inserted by pointing it toward the rear of the aircraft. Then a bight, or loop, is formed in the static line and held at eye level. The parachutist does not release the bight until he moves into the door.

"Check static lines" is the fifth jump command. This is a plural command, because there are several static lines attached to the anchor-line cable. The hand signal begins at eye level, with the thumb and index finger of each hand forming an O. The jumpmaster extends and joins his remaining fingers, with the palms facing in. As he gives the oral command, he extends his arms to the front until the elbows are nearly locked, then returns to the starting position. He repeats the arm-and-hand signal at least three times, ensuring the knife edges of his hands are toward the parachutists and the palms face each other.

After repeating this command, each parachutist checks his static line and the static line of the parachutist to the front. Each parachutist checks visually and by feeling with his free hand. He does not release the bight for checks. He verifies the following items:

- Static-line snap hook is properly attached to the anchor-line cable with the safety wire properly inserted. Static line is free of frays and tears.

- Static line is not misrouted and is properly stowed on pack tray.

- All excess slack in the static line is taken up and stowed in the static-line slack retainer.

- Pack closing tie is routed through the pack opening loop.

- Pack tray is intact.

The last two jumpers in each stick face about. The next-to-last jumper inspects the last jumper's static line and gives him a sharp tap to indicate that the static line and pack tray have been checked and are safe for jumping. Each parachutist gives the parachutist to the front a sharp tap, signifying that the static line and pack tray have been checked and are safe for jumping.

"Check equipment" is the sixth jump command. The jumpmaster starts this arm-and-hand signal with the fingertips centered on his chest, palms facing the chest, and fingers and thumb of each hand extended and joined; or with his arms extended to the sides at shoulder level, fingers and thumbs extended and joined, and palms facing toward the parachutists. He gives the oral command, extends his arms to the sides at shoulder level, and then returns them to the chest; or bends his arms at the elbows, bringing the fingertips to the center of the chest, and then returns to the extended position. He repeats the arm-and-hand signal at least three times. The jumpmaster must check his own equipment.

After repeating this command, each parachutist checks his equipment, starting at the helmet, and ensures there are no sharp edges on the rim of the ballistic helmet and that the chin strap and parachutist retention straps are properly routed and secured. The parachutist then physically seats the activating lever of the chest-strap ejector snap and the leg-strap ejector snaps. If jumping with combat equipment, the parachutist also ensures the ejector snap of the hooked pile tape (HPT) lowering line is properly attached and seated. The parachutist completes these actions with the free hand while maintaining a firm grip on the static line bight with the other hand.

"Sound off for equipment check" is the seventh jump command. As he gives the oral command, the jumpmaster cups his hands and places the thumbs behind the ears.

After everybody repeats this command in unison, the last parachutist in the outboard stick sounds off, saying "Okay," and gives the parachutist in front a sharp tap on the thigh or buttocks.

The signal is continued until it gets to the first jumper in the stick, who notifies the jumpmaster by extending his free hand toward the jumpmaster and saying, "All okay, jumpmaster." He will not lower his hand until the jumpmaster has acknowledged the report by slapping the jumper's open palm.

For a C-130 aircraft, this signal is passed to the number-twenty-five parachutist (just forward of the wheel well), who forms a circle with his index finger and thumb of his free hand, turns toward the center of the aircraft, and gives the okay signal to number twenty-four (the last parachutist of the inboard stick). The tap and indication that all previous parachutists are okay is passed up to number four, the first parachutist of the inboard stick, who signals number three, first parachutist to the rear of the wheel well. The signal is continued until it gets to the number-one parachutist, who notifies the jumpmaster by pointing to the jumpmaster and saying, "All okay."

A parachutist who has an equipment problem notifies the jumpmaster, assistant jumpmaster, or safety personnel by raising his outboard hand high above the anchor-line cable, palm facing the jumpmaster. The parachutists do not pass this signal. The jumpmaster, assistant jumpmaster, or safety either corrects the deficiency or removes the parachutist from the stick.

"One minute" is the second time warning. The jumpmaster shouts the command and holds up his inboard arm with index finger extended. The jumpers repeat the command and signal over the shoulder closest to the skin of the aircraft.

"Thirty seconds" is the next warning. The jumpmaster shouts this command and holds his inboard hand up with thumb and forefinger held about an inch apart. The jumpers repeat this command and signal.

"Stand by" is the eighth jump command. The jumpmaster gives this command about ten seconds before the aircraft reaches the release point and only after the aircraft has cleared all obstacles near the drop zone (DZ). Starting with his hands at the shoulders, the jumpmaster extends and joins his index and middle fingers, curling the remaining fingers and thumb of each hand toward the palm. He extends his arms down to the sides at a forty-five-degree angle by locking the elbows, and points to both doors at the same time.

At this command, the jumpers repeat the command and the lead parachutist shuffles toward the door, estab-

lishes eye contact with the "safety" (an assistant jumpmaster acting as a safety officer), hands the safety his static line, holds his elbows firmly into his sides with his palms on the end of the reserve, turns and centers himself in the open jump door, and awaits the command "Go."

All following parachutists maintain the static-line bight and close up behind the preceding parachutist. The two jumpers behind the lead jumper are at one arm's distance, with elbow locked. All remaining jumpers shuffle forward until their reserve parachute is touching the main parachute in front of them.

"Go" is the ninth jump command. The green light is the final time warning on air force aircraft. It tells the jumpmaster that as far as the aircrew is concerned, conditions are safe and it is time to issue the "Go" command. The jumpmaster gives the verbal command "Go" and may also signal the first parachutist out with a sharp tap on the thigh. If the jumpmaster is to use this signal, he will have explained it during his briefing.

At the command "Go," the first parachutist exits the aircraft. All subsequent jumpers begin moving toward the door, using a shuffle. Once the jumpers begin to shuffle, they assume an elbow-locked position with the arm that is controlling their static line. Each jumper places his static-line control hand so that it is nearly touching the back of the pack tray of the jumper in front of him. This establishes the proper jump interval. Jumpers do not place their static-line control hand in a position so that it extends past the pack tray of the jumper in front of them.

As each jumper approaches the door, he establishes eye contact with the safety and hands his static line to the safety. Once the safety has control of the jumper's static line, the jumper returns his hand to the end of the reserve parachute with his fingers spread.

After handing his static line to the safety in the vicinity of the lead edge of the door, the jumper executes a left or right turn (as appropriate) and faces directly toward and centered on the door with both hands over the ends of the reserve parachute, fingers spread. He continues the momentum of his movement by walking toward the door, focusing on the horizon, and stepping on the jump platform. He pushes off with either foot and vigorously jumps up and out, away from the aircraft. He immediately snaps into a good, tight-body position and exaggerates the bend into his hips to form an L shape.

Students are making a mass exit from the thirty-four-foot tower, as observed from the base of the tower, looking upward. During tower week the training emphasis shifts from individual actions to mass, or group, actions. Mass-exit procedures teach the students how to exit the aircraft as quickly and safely as possible.
Hans Halberstadt

A student is demonstrating a good body position on exit. His hands are on the sides of his reserve, his chin is tucked, his body is bent at the waist, and his feet and knees are held together. This body position keeps the jumper from tumbling in the slipstream outside the aircraft and helps mitigate opening shock. *Gregory Mast*

All these commands and jumper actions are rehearsed during tower week mock-door training. Extra instructors will be on hand to evaluate and coach the students.

Jump-refusal procedures are also covered during this period of instruction. A jump refusal is defined as a jumper in the door who refuses three commands to exit the aircraft. Students receive the textbook lecture on procedures, which is generally followed by real-world words of wisdom from the Black Hats. The best time to refuse a jump is before you get on board the aircraft.

If a jumper stops or hesitates in the door, he will be given the command "Green light, go" three times, accompanied by a sharp tap to the thigh with each repetition of the command. If the jumper does not exit, the jumpmaster will tell him, "You are a jump refusal, and I am taking you out of the door." The jumpmaster will grab the parachutist from the rear and take him forward in the aircraft. The jump refusal will be seated and given the command "Do not touch your equipment." This is a legal order, and the jump refusal, regardless of rank, will be punished under the Uniform Code of Military Justice for any violation of this order. Once the aircraft has landed, the situation will be sorted out

administratively, which at BAC means the student who refused to jump will be dropped from the course.

THIRTY-FOUR-FOOT TOWER, PART TWO

The thirty-four-foot tower, like the mock-door trainer, was part of the training syllabus during ground week. During tower week, students use the thirty-four-foot towers at Tower Branch to rehearse mass exits, simulate parachute malfunctions, and become familiarized with jumping combat equipment. Students are critiqued during these exercises and will receive a "go" or "no go" evaluation. Students must receive a satisfactory evaluation on the towers before being allowed to advance to jump week.

The thirty-four-foot tower has two doors, a right and a left. During mass-exit training, four students exit each door at one-second intervals. Students execute the first three points of performance (proper exit, check body position, and count; check canopy and immediately gain canopy control; and keep a sharp lookout for all jumpers during your entire descent), just as they did during ground week.

Parachute malfunctions are simulated in order to teach students the procedures for activating their reserve parachutes. Prior to exiting the tower, students will be informed of the type of malfunction, total or partial, and what actions to take. This training is repetitive, and it drills the procedures into the students until they become instinctual. Two reserve parachute types are in use at BAC, so students must be trained in activation procedures for both types.

The modified improved reserve parachute system (MIRPS) is the older of the two types and is being phased out for safety reasons. The MIRPS can be identified by the location of the ripcord grip, on the right side of the parachute pack. The primary method of activating this parachute is called the pull-drop method. The reason that this is called the pull-drop method is because the parachutist pulls the ripcord handle and then drops the handle, so that his hands will be free to control the canopy during descent. Using the pull-drop, the parachutist keeps a tight body position with feet and knees together, grasps the left carrying handle of the reserve parachute with his left hand, turns his head left or right, and pulls the ripcord grip with his right hand.

The soft-loop center-pull (SLCP) reserve can be identified by the upward-facing ripcord grip on the center of the parachute pack. The SLCP requires less effort to activate and, unlike the MIRPS, may be activated with either hand. This is particularly advantageous if the jumper is injured upon exit. The primary method for activation is also the pull-drop method, with some variation. The jumper may use either hand to pull the ripcord and does not need to grip the parachute pack with the other hand. However, at BAC, students are taught to grasp the pack tray with their left hand, in the same manner as the MIRPS, when activating the SLCP reserve.

Students are familiarized with the procedures for jumping with combat gear during tower week. They will be rigged with an all-purpose lightweight individual carrying equipment (ALICE) pack and M1950 weapons case on a modified quick-release system. After executing the third point of performance, the student unties the M1950 and releases the suspended ALICE pack to simulate lowering the gear during a real jump. This is done before the student reaches the mound at the end of the ride.

COMMON ERRORS STUDENTS MAKE DURING TOWER WEEK

There are several mistakes that students frequently commit during tower week. Advance knowledge of these common errors may help you avoid them. They include:

- Failure to maintain a one-second interval between jumpers. This includes both hesitation in the door and overeager students rushing to exit.

- Using improper body position on exit. This can be caused by rushing, student fear, or improper training. Some common mistakes include improper placement of hands on the reserve parachute ("puppy dogging" or putting hands on top of the reserve instead of on its sides with fingers spread), feet and knees apart, and failure to maintain a tight body tuck.

- Improper exit and falling out of the door. Improper exits are usually weak exits, when the student fails to make a vigorous step up and out the door.

(Right) Students are waiting to receive evaluations of their performance on the thirty-four-foot tower. Students who receive a "No Go" evaluation may be recycled to the next class or dropped from the course altogether, so there is some apprehension during these evaluations. *Gregory Mast*

During tower week students learn to exit the thirty-four-foot towers with combat equipment. This exercise familiarizes students with the procedures for jumping with combat equipment as well as the restrictions placed on their movement by this gear. *Hans Halberstadt*

Students make a mass exit from the thirty-four-foot tower with combat equipment. In addition to rehearsing points of performance and malfunctions, they must also drop the equipment prior to reaching the end of the cable. *Gregory Mast*

Students executing malfunction drills are activating their reserve parachutes using the pull-drop method after their four thousand count, simulating either a total or partial malfunction as directed by the Black Hats. *Gregory Mast*

Another view of students exiting the thirty-four-foot tower. Note the students waiting in the stairwells leading to the top of the tower. *Hans Halberstadt*

• Failing to count. The importance of counting cannot be overemphasized. Failure to count can turn a survivable malfunction or failure into a fatal situation.

SUSPENDED-HARNESS TRAINING

While the suspended-harness trainer is not technically classed as a medieval instrument of torture, some students might think otherwise. This training apparatus allows students to practice actions taken during the third and fourth points of performance that deal with canopy control and landing procedures. Much like the thirty-four-foot tower, this apparatus also reinforces the value of a correctly fitted parachute harness in a lesson that is not as sudden but much more prolonged.

The suspended-harness trainer is a modified troop parachute harness suspended from a spreader bar assembly by four web risers. The spreader bars simulate canopy reaction to riser manipulation much the same as the T10

This student is demonstrating how not to exit the tower. He is looking at the ground, has incorrect hand placement, and his feet and knees are not together. He is also in for a surprise at opening shock given the placement of his ALICE pack. *Hans Halberstadt*

A Black Hat is adjusting a student's gear for suspended-harness training. Instructors constantly monitor equipment for safety and serviceability. *Gregory Mast*

A student is listening to instruction during suspended-harness training. The students will be presented with various scenarios and are evaluated on their responses, such as estimation of the direction of wind drift and correct riser slips. *Gregory Mast*

Students are in the suspended-harness trainer (SHT), which simulates the control functions of the risers on a T10 parachute. One student is in the harness, and another assists during the uncomfortable process of learning to control a parachute canopy. *Gregory Mast*

canopy. There are two formal periods of instruction on the suspended-harness trainer. During the first session, students learn to execute two-riser slips (left, right, front, and rear) in response to wind drift and observed conditions on the drop zone and how to assume a proper landing attitude. During the second session, students learn to execute single-riser diagonal slips, procedures for emergency landings (such as in trees, water, and wire), and how to react to twists, collisions, and entanglements.

SWING-LANDING TRAINER

The swing-landing trainer raises the ante on the suspended-harness trainer by adding motion and parachute-landing falls. This apparatus consists of a rather elaborate system of pulleys and lines that simulate downward motion and oscillation similar to that while under the canopy and allows the students to practice parachute landing falls under these conditions. Students step off of a platform twelve feet above the ground to initiate the swinging action. This swing is modified by the instructors using a control line and by the student using riser slips. The instructor controls the rate of descent and dictates the type of PLF to be executed by the student.

A student is using an alternate method of activating the canopy-release assembly during suspended-harness training. *Gregory Mast*

A student prepares to step off the platform of the swing-landing trainer, which simulates the oscillation and motion of a parachute canopy during landing. Students practice canopy control and parachute landing falls (PLFs) on this device. *Hans Halberstadt*

Students have two learning objectives on the swing-landing trainer. The first is how to assume correct landing attitude under different circumstances. The second is how to execute front, side, and rear parachute landing falls while descending and oscillating under a simulated canopy.

250-FOOT TOWER

The 250-foot towers are probably the most easily recognized landmark at Fort Benning. Three of the four original towers remain, looming over Tower Branch like giant red and white insects. Contrary to the old legend, they were not purchased from the New York World's Fair or from Coney Island Amusement Park, although they both had a ride called the Parachute Drop. This urban legend was debunked largely by retired 1st Sgt. Ed Howard, an army history enthusiast and former Black Hat. According to Sergeant Howard, four towers were designed and constructed specifically for the new airborne training program in 1942. One was destroyed by a tornado in 1953.

The towers are designed to familiarize students with descent under a modified T10 canopy. Each tower has four arms, which hoist a circular metal frame to which the canopy is attached. The student dangles in a harness under the canopy as it is hoisted to the top of the arm, enjoying the view if he can while responding to commands from the ground. Once stopped at the top, the jumper is "jogged" loose to drift back down to Eubanks Field. Generally speaking, when the towers are used, only three of the four arms are utilized, because one arm is facing into the wind and the jumper would be blown into the tower if he were dropped from that arm. Sadly, not every class gets to use the towers due to operational reasons, so consider yourself lucky if you get to make a drop from the 250-foot tower.

PARACHUTE MALFUNCTIONS

The class on parachute malfunctions is the last period of formal instruction at BAC and marks the transition between the ground phase of training and the

The SLT utilizes a fairly elaborate series of lines and pulleys in order to create the simulation of a descending canopy. The Black Hats control the motion and the rate of descent by a control line. *Hans Halberstadt*

Black Hats control the student's swing and descent by use of a control line. As the student swings back and forth, the Black Hat on the control line gives him instructions and evaluates him on how well he responds to those instructions. *Gregory Mast*

The swing-landing trainer provides realistic training for parachute-landing falls. Like the lateral drift apparatus, the landing surface for the SLT is gravel, which is considered a "soft" surface. Despite the soft surface, many students experience bone-jarring landings, just like under a real canopy. *Gregory Mast*

jump phase. It is a mark of achievement to make it to this class, given on the last day of tower week. During the introduction of the class, the Black Hats instruct the students to look to their right and their left and take note of those who are absent. The class is given in the same area as the airborne orientation and, conditions permitting, the 250-foot tower is rigged with four dummies (mannequins, not dimwitted volunteers) to demonstrate the types of malfunctions students hope they never encounter. The sound of a dummy impacting the earth is enough to silence

(Right) A student on the SLT prepares to land by pulling on risers. The direction of the PLF is dictated by the Black Hat on the control line. *Hans Halberstadt*

THE ROCK

"I went through the Basic Airborne Course in October and November 1978, right out of basic and infantry training. All this training was right here on Fort Benning, without a break between one course and another. There were a few surprises: First, it seemed easier than the training we'd just gone through. Those of us just out of the Eleven Bravo course were in great shape, so the PT was not demanding at all. Second, it was a bit of a shock to be mixed in with people from all across the army and even the other branches of service—marines, sailors, airmen. There were women in the course, too, and the ages and levels of physical fitness were quite different than we had become accustomed to. Some of these people fell out of the runs, another surprise to those of us just out of advanced infantry training (AIT).

"October was a good time to go through the course—nice cool mornings, and not too much heat later in the day. Instruction today is basically the same as then; the "snap and pop" of the Black Hats was very impressive, and the quality of each block of training was (and still is) superb. Everything was clearly precise and well-rehearsed, just as it is today. Even the longer runs were not challenging by the standards of the infantry program we'd just been through.

"Most of the training wasn't tough, but I almost failed the swing landing trainer. One of the Black Hats made it clear I was on borrowed time, and if I couldn't do it right, I would get a 'no go.' He took a small rock and said, 'Put this between your feet and keep it there.' I did as he told me, and kept my feet and knees properly together and passed the block of instruction.
I picked up that rock and kept it—and still have it!"

—1st Sgt. Ed Howard, USA (Ret.)

A student drags himself away from the swing-landing trainer after a hard landing and gets ready for his next try. Although landings on the SLT can be rough, students rarely incur a serious injury during this training. *Hans Halberstadt*

Swing-landing training is performance oriented. This means that students are evaluated and given a "go" or "no go" rating. A "go" evaluation is required to move to the next phase of training. *Hans Halberstadt*

Student on the platform of the swing-landing trainer, immediately prior to stepping off into the air. *Hans Halberstadt*

The last period of formal instruction at BAC is the class on parachute malfunctions. The class is given in the same area as the airborne orientation, the first class the students receive at BAC. Here, a dummy is dropped from the 250-foot tower to demonstrate the "cigarette roll" parachute malfunction. The dummy drop opens the class, and the loud thud it makes on impact gets the students' total attention. *Gregory Mast*

any student chatter in the bleachers and is a grim reminder that parachuting is an inherently hazardous activity.

Although equipment failures and malfunctions are relatively rare, they do happen, and jumpers are killed if they cannot diagnose and react to these situations correctly. During this class, students receive instruction on how to react to parachute malfunctions, total and partial. They are also instructed on towed jumper procedures, how to correct twisted suspension lines, and how to react to collisions and entanglements with other jumpers on descent.

A total parachute malfunction is defined as the failure of the parachute to open or to deploy. Total malfunctions are rare, but they do happen. They can be caused by a severed static line, a broken snap hook, or a broken anchor-line cable-all extremely rare occurrences. The most likely cause is when a jumper gets stuck on stupid and forgets to hook up or hooks up incorrectly. Perhaps he has neglected to check his static line when instructed to do so, or his buddy has screwed up the equipment check.

Students are taught from day one the four thousand count, repeated like a mantra until it becomes second, third, and fourth nature. If they do not feel an opening

shock by the time they have finished the four thousand count after leaving the aircraft, they are to immediately activate their reserve parachute. There is little time to spare before the ground interrupts your fall in this situation, which is the reason for the count. As the old saying goes, it's not the fall, but landing, that alters social standing.

A "cigarette roll" or "streamer" is not technically a total malfunction, but the parachutist must react as though it were, by immediately deploying the reserve. In this instance, the canopy has been pulled from the deployment bag but does not inflate as the jumper plummets toward the ground. This malfunction occurs when a portion of the skirt blows between two suspension lines and begins to roll with the opposite fabric. The heat generated by the friction of the fabric being rolled causes the nylon to fuse and blocks the air channel in the canopy.

There are four types of partial parachute malfunctions. They are a complete inversion, semi-inversion, blown section or gore, and broken suspension lines. Corrective actions for each of these malfunctions are slightly different.

A complete inversion is basically a parachute that opens inside out, often due to a rigging problem. This malfunction may occur when a portion of the skirt blows inward between a pair of suspension lines on the opposite side of the parachute. The canopy turns inside out with no decrease in its lifting surface. A complete inversion may be difficult to detect if it occurs during initial deployment. There may be no need to activate the reserve unless the canopy was damaged during inversion. Although the parachute failed to function properly, it can take the jumper safely to the ground. However, the inversion may increase the rate of descent. If the jumper's rate of descent is greater than that of other jumpers, it is time to activate the reserve parachute.

A semi-inversion is a when the canopy is fouled by a suspension line running over the canopy, creating two smaller lobes. During World War II this malfunction was nicknamed a "Mae West," in reference to the actress' legendary bust size. Of course, nowadays only students who are film buffs would get that reference, so instructors now tell students that if their canopy looks like butt cheeks, they have a semi-inversion. The anti-inversion net on the T10D is designed to reduce the occurrence of this type of malfunction. This malfunction may remain stable, become completely inverted, or revert to normal during descent. The total lifting capability of the canopy is decreased by the formation of a secondary lobe, with a corresponding increase in the rate of descent. The canopy and suspension lines may also be burned by friction and weakened during descent. A jumper confronted with a semi-inversion must activate the reserve parachute.

A parachute may be damaged on opening by the stress of speed and weight, with portions of the canopy ripping or falling off. This is referred to as a blown section or gore malfunction. When this happens, a panel, section, or gore is ripped or torn out, resulting in one or more holes in the canopy. Students are taught to look for holes larger than their ballistic helmets, and they are taught how to distinguish a hole from a patch. When canopies are repaired, the patches are a different color from the canopy, with regular

A dummy is dropped from the 250-foot tower with a parachute exhibiting semi-inversion malfunction. A semi-inversion occurs when a suspension line runs over the top of the canopy, dividing it into smaller lobes. Note the inverted suspension lines inside the red circle. *Gregory Mast*

A dummy is dropped from the 250-foot tower to demonstrate use of the reserve parachute. Note the position of the dummy, due to the fact that the point of suspension for the reserve parachute is the chest and not the shoulders. *Gregory Mast*

edges and seams. Patches are never blue and ragged. That would be a hole. Students have been known to mistake a patch for a hole and needlessly activate their reserve.

The jumper visually inspects the canopy, then compares his rate of descent with that of others around him. If he detects holes, and his rate of descent is greater than that of other jumpers, he must deploy the reserve parachute.

The fourth type of partial malfunction is broken suspension lines. At BAC, students learn that six or more broken suspension lines are enough to create an increased rate of descent. If a jumper's rate of descent is greater than those around him, he must activate his reserve parachute.

During the second point of performance, each paratrooper checks his canopy after it deploys, looking for holes, tears, rips, or any other damage that may have occurred during opening shock. Here, the Black Hats demonstrate the differences between holes in a canopy and patches. Inexperienced jumpers have confused the two and deployed their reserve parachutes upon seeing patches in their main canopy. *Gregory Mast*

BAC students are instructed to err on the side of caution in the event of malfunctions. If there is any uncertainty, they should activate their reserve parachute. When in doubt, whip it out.

Jumpmasters brief parachutists on the towed jumper scenario before every jump, as part of the sustained airborne training script. It is a rare situation but extremely dangerous, one that the jumper can make fatal. Although that scenario is not classed as a parachute malfunction, a parachutist can be towed behind the aircraft by a misrouted static line or by a piece of equipment that has snagged the aircraft during the jumper's exit. During the four thousand count, the jumper will feel an excessive opening shock and then feel himself being towed by the aircraft. The ride will be bumpy, to say the least, and the jumper may be battered against the aircraft by the slipstream and prop blast. The difference between life and death may be the jumper's ability to remain calm and think clearly.

There will be a very uncomfortable time for the jumper as he is dragged across the sky, while decisions are being made inside the aircraft. During that time, the jumper remains in a tight body position, protecting his ripcord grip until he is either retrieved inside the aircraft or is cut free by the loadmaster on the pilot's order. The jumper should try to keep his eyes open, if possible.

Under no circumstances must a jumper activate his reserve parachute prior to being cut away or pulled inside the aircraft. Accidental activation of the reserve while the jumper is being towed will almost certainly result in the death of the jumper.

If the decision is made to retrieve the jumper inside the aircraft, the jumper remains in a tight body position until he is completely inside the aircraft. A towed jumper must not use his hands to assist the retrieving personnel. The most important action of a towed jumper is to protect his ripcord grip. Once safely on board the aircraft, the jumper may require medical attention. He

will most likely have to endure jokes about soiled under-garments as well.

If the jumper is cut free of the aircraft, the main parachute may or may not deploy. If the jumper was towed by something other than the static line, the main parachute will deploy and inflate. There is no need to activate the reserve parachute. If the jumper was towed by the static line and is cut free, the jumper must immediately deploy his reserve using the pull-drop method.

Twisted suspension lines, referred to as a "twist," are not a parachute malfunction, but it is a situation that demands corrective action on the part of the jumper for his own safety. The jumper will detect a twist when he executes the second point of performance (check canopy and gain canopy control). The main parachute may have twisted suspension lines, risers, or both. This condition may be caused by a single action or a combination of actions. The most common causes include:

- The deployment bag spinning before the canopy deploys

- The canopy spinning when it comes out of the deployment bag and before it inflates

- The parachutist tumbling or spinning (caused by improper exit and body position) during his descent

If the suspension lines are twisted and the parachutist cannot raise his head enough to check the canopy properly, he compares his rate of descent with that of nearby para-chutists. If his descent is the same as other jumpers around him, he untwists his suspension lines by reaching behind his neck, grasping each pair of risers, and exerting an outward pull on each pair. He kicks his legs in a bicycle motion, continues to pull outward on the risers, and kicks until the twists are out of the suspension lines. When the twists are out of the lines, he checks the canopy and gains canopy control.

Although not technically a parachute malfunction, entangled jumpers are a hazard of mass tactical jumps. When two jumpers' parachutes become entangled, it can lead to serious injury or death if the two jumpers do not work together as a team. Here, Black Hats demonstrate the procedures for entangled jumpers on how to disengage one another if possible, and how to land if still entangled. *Gregory Mast*

Collisions and entanglements are hazards presented by the crowded sky of mass tactical jumps. Parachutists are instructed to keep at least fifty feet of separation from other jumpers and always attempt to slip or turn away to avoid collisions. If unable to avoid a collision, he uses the spread-eagle method to bounce off another canopy or suspension lines. If a parachutist enters another parachutist's suspension lines, the entering parachutist assumes the modified position of attention, with the right hand protecting (but not grasping) the ripcord grip, in the hope that he will exit the same location without becoming entangled. If not, the entering parachutist may use his left hand to assist in exiting the other jumper's canopy and suspension lines the same way he entered.

If parachutists become entangled, their actions required to correct the problem depend upon the type of parachute used. For the T10D parachutes used as BAC, the higher parachutist moves hand-under-hand down to the lower parachutist. They attempt to establish eye contact and hold onto each other by the left main lift web(s). They must not touch the other jumper's canopy-release assemblies. They decide which parachute landing fall to execute upon contact with the ground, and both parachutists execute the same PLF. If they are face-to-face, they will not execute a front PLF. If they are back-to-back, they will not execute a rear PLF. If one parachutist has a completely inflated canopy, neither parachutist activates the reserve parachute. If both parachutes lose lift capabilities, parachutists use the pull-crop method to activate their reserve parachutes.

Procedures for reserve parachutes that are accidentally deployed inside the aircraft are also covered in this class. An accidentally deployed reserve can be a potentially fatal situation for the jumper who owns the reserve and for those between him and the door. The vacuum created by an open door in flight will suck the parachute out faster than you think possible and will drag a jumper in harness through whatever is between him and the door. That includes the skin of the aircraft near the door. If the deployment occurs forward of the wheel well, the affected jumper and those around him should try to grab or step on the canopy to keep it from catching air and going out the door. If the deployment occurs aft of the wheel well, toward the door, it is unlikely that the canopy can be smothered. In that instance, the best advice for the jumper is to follow the canopy out the door as quickly as possible.

FIVE

Airborne students are taught to remove the troop parachute harness and reserve parachute while lying on their back. After the PLF is complete, the parachutist activates one canopy-release assembly to deflate the canopy and prevent him from being dragged across the DZ. Then he removes his equipment before getting up to retrieve the parachute.

Jump Week: Stand By

BAC students must make one "night" jump in order to graduate. During the summer months, the night jumps are often twilight or sunset jumps, due to long daylight hours and a compressed training schedule. Here, two students prepare to land at Fryar Drop Zone. *Gregory Mast*

You've made it to jump week. Now the only thing that stands between you and your jump wings is five jumps from a high-performance aircraft at an altitude of 1,250 feet above ground level. The training schedule for jump week is the most hectic and unpredictable of the three weeks at BAC because several key variables are beyond the control of the cadre. Weather and operational readiness issues, such as aircraft availability and maintenance, drive the schedule for the final week of training.

An airborne student descends under a T10 parachute at Fryar Drop Zone, Fort Benning. The T10 has been in service since the 1950s, with modifications. The current version used at Fort Benning is the T10D. *Gregory Mast*

Training during jump week takes place at Lawson Field and at Fryar Drop Zone. Here is where students put to the test all that they have learned in the previous two weeks. The U.S. Army has five standards by which it judges the validity of airborne training, as outlined in FM 3-21.220, *Static Line Parachuting Techniques and Tactics:*

• Strict discipline

• High standards of proficiency on each training apparatus and during each phase of training

• A vigorous physical conditioning program to ensure parachutists are capable of jumping with a minimum risk of injury

• A strong sense of esprit de corps and camaraderie among parachutists

• Emphasis on developing mental alertness, instantaneous execution of commands, self-confidence, and confidence in the equipment

McCarthy Hall at Lawson Army Airfield is located about a mile or so southwest of Ground and Tower Branch. The original McCarthy Hall was demolished by accident, but the new hall is on the same historic location that has been in constant use since the very first day of airborne training at Fort Benning. This is where students will draw their gear, conduct sustained airborne training, receive jumpmaster personnel inspections (JMPI), and spend many an uncomfortable hour in a harness, waiting to board the jump aircraft.

Fryar Drop Zone is located on the Alabama side of Fort Benning. The drop zone is 2,500 yards long by 1,300 yards wide and is surrounded by forests and water hazards. Every jump week, a number of particularly talented students get to test their tree-landing and water-landing skills, although the vast majority of jumpers manage to land in this large drop zone (DZ). Bleachers are set up at the eastern edge of the drop zone, where friends and families of the students may observe the jump operations.

The training objectives for students are defined in the program of instruction, broken down by week. However, the objectives for jump week do not really describe what happens during that week. Getting a class of students out of a C-130 over the drop zone is a long and complex process at BAC. A typical jump week requires a student to complete five jumps, one being a night jump, in four days, with graduation ceremonies and out-possessing taking place on the final day of the week. These are four very long and exhausting days for students and cadre alike, if everything goes well.

During jump week each student is expected to:

- Correctly don and adjust the T10 parachute, MIRPS/SLCP reserve, and combat equipment. Students will be instructed in the correct methods of rigging their combat equipment using the harness single point release system.

- Respond to jump commands while inside an aircraft

- Control body position after jumping from an aircraft until parachute opening shock

- Control the parachute during descent

- Execute a parachute landing fall

- Control the parachute upon landing while making five parachute jumps from an air force aircraft at an altitude of 1,250 feet

What this means is that the student is expected to demonstrate a reasonable level of proficiency in the basic skills of military parachuting. In real terms it means that the student can exit the aircraft safely, without injuring himself or other jumpers; navigate a crowded sky under a nonsteerable canopy without creating a hazard to other jumpers; land without injuring himself too badly; assemble his kit; and exit the drop zone in a military manner. The key theme is to avoid injury whenever possible. An injured paratrooper is a liability to his unit and represents a reduction in the combat effectiveness of the unit before the mission begins. Unlike a civilian drop zone, a military drop zone is where the mission starts, not where it ends.

Students on board a Lockheed C-130 are hooked up and waiting for "Go." This is a daylight jump, with combat equipment. Note that they maintain the correct interval between jumpers by extending the arm controlling the static line. *Photo by BAC cadre*

Students land at Fryar Drop Zone following a mass exit with combat equipment. They lower their ALICE packs and M1950 weapons cases on the HPT line at about two hundred feet above ground level. The T10's anti-inversion netting is clearly visible on the canopy in the foreground. *Gregory Mast*

TYPICAL JUMP SCHEDULE

The first jump at BAC is a "Hollywood" jump, with students conducting individual exits. "Hollywood" is slang for a jump made without combat equipment and implies a joy ride. On the first jump, only one door of the aircraft is used at a time, alternating between starboard and port sides each pass over the DZ. This procedure is referred to as ADEPT option one (alternate door exit procedures for training).

The second jump is made with combat equipment, with students conducting individual exits. ADEPT option two is used on this jump, in which both doors of the aircraft will be used during a single pass over the DZ. Initially, the jumpmaster will exit one stick from the primary door. The assistant jumpmaster will wait until only three jumpers remain in that stick before issuing the eighth jump command to his stick, waiting until the final jumper from the first stick exits before issuing the command "Go" to his stick.

The third jump is Hollywood mass exits. During this type of exit, parachutists may exit from both doors at the same time. The jumpmaster gives the command "Go," and the assistant jumpmaster then turns and gives his jumper the command "Go" to create a staggered effect.

The fourth jump is mass exits with combat equipment.

The fifth, and final, jump is a mass-exit night jump with combat equipment. During the summer months, the "night" jump is really more of a "twilight" jump, because the compressed schedule of jump week will not permit delaying the jump until total darkness.

This schedule is typical, meaning that there may be some variation in the order of jumps. Some classes might have the night jump as their fourth rather than fifth jump. Although there is only one jump under night conditions, some Black Hats joke that most students' first three jumps are night jumps because their eyes are closed when they leave the airplane. According to the Black Hats, the first jump is the safest, because students tend to

execute every action as taught. The second jump is the scariest for the students, because they have a real idea of the hazards one encounters upon leaving an aircraft in flight. The greatest number of injuries occurs on the fourth and fifth jumps, because students tend to get cocky, and they have just enough knowledge to be dangerous and not enough experience to know better.

RIGGING COMBAT EQUIPMENT FOR PARACHUTING

The paratrooper's real job starts after landing on the drop zone. Given the nature of airborne operations, a paratrooper needs to jump with enough combat equipment and weapons to be self-sufficient upon landing, due to the possibility of being scattered during the air drop. This necessity to carry a great deal of extra weight adds complexity and danger to operations that are already hazardous. At BAC, students learn how to rig an ALICE pack and a weapon-a soldier's basic combat load-for jump operations. Students do not jump with body armor or load-bearing equipment.

The ALICE pack is slung beneath the reserve parachute by a quick-release system called a harness, single-point release (HSPR, for those keeping track of the military acronyms). It is an *H*-shaped harness that suspends the combat load from the jumper's parachute harness. The HSPR is attached to the D-rings on the main lift web outside of the connector snaps of the reserve parachute. It has leg straps that stabilize the pack during movement in the aircraft, exit, and main-parachute deployment. When correctly rigged, it has a tab that will release the pack and leg straps from the jumper when it is pulled.

The pack and M1950 weapons case are attached to the jumper by a lowering line, called a hook-pile tape lowering line (HPT). It is a fifteen-foot length of tubular nylon with a stow pocket that secures the folded line by hook-and-pile fasteners. The HPT suspends the jumper's combat equipment and weapon below him during landing. This substantial load dangling beneath a jumper under a canopy also poses a threat to other jumpers if its owner is careless and does not pay attention to the situation around him.

The M1950 weapons case is another piece of equipment that has been in the inventory for a very long time, as evidenced by its nomenclature. It is a padded case, adjustable in length to accommodate a variety of individual weapons. It is attached to the left side of the jumper by a quick-release snap and stabilized by tie-downs.

A student demonstrates combat equipment rigged for parachute operations. The ALICE pack is slung below the reserve parachute by a quick-release harness and is attached to the jumper by a lowering line. The roster number on this student's helmet indicates that he is an officer (or an Alpha, in Black Hat jargon), and the patch on his right sleeve indicates that he was in combat with the 1st Cavalry Division. *Hans Halberstadt*

Students conduct mass exits from both doors of a Lockheed C-130 over Fryar Drop Zone, utilizing the ADEPT method. ADEPT is the acronym for alternate-door exit procedures for training, which is used to minimize the potential for jumper collisions when using both doors of the aircraft over a drop zone. *Gregory Mast*

A closer view of a student preparing to land with combat equipment lowered on the HPT line. The quick-release harness can be seen dangling from the ALICE pack. *Gregory Mast*

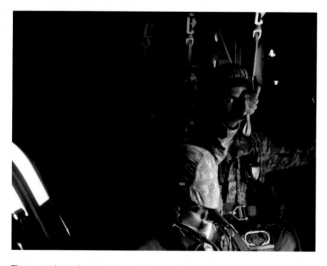

These students have their static lines attached to the aircraft's anchor cable. The universal static-line hook is attached, with the opening toward the outboard side of the aircraft. *Photo by BAC cadre*

Students jump with a dummy M16 or M4 rifle, called a "rubber ducky" because the replica weapon is composed primarily of high-density plastic.

When the jumper reaches an altitude of two hundred feet above the drop zone, he will prepare to lower combat equipment as part of the fourth point of performance (slip or turn into the wind and prepare to land). The jumper already will have loosened the equipment tie-downs on the M1950 as part of the third point of performance. At two hundred feet, the jumper will look around him and below him for other jumpers. If it is clear, then he will pull the release handle on the HSPR, which will free the suspended ALICE pack. The pack will drop and dangle under the jumper on the lowering line. The jumper will then activate the quick-release snap on the weapons case and send that down the lowering line. The pack and weapons case will impact the ground first, generally a short distance from the jumper's point of impact.

Upon landing, the student will begin the equipment recovery process. He will roll onto his back and release one canopy-release assembly, then remove his harness and reserve parachute. While remaining on his back, he will drag the pack and weapons case to himself by the lowering line. Prior to getting on one knee to begin canopy retrieval, he will open the weapons case and engage his weapon.

STATIC-LINE PARACHUTING

The basic techniques for mass tactical airborne operations have changed little since they were developed before and during World War II. One of the earliest developments was the static line that is used to deploy the paratrooper's main canopy. This simple technique is reliable and almost fool-proof when used as directed (never underestimate the ability of some soldiers to screw up). Special operations forces routinely employ more advanced parachuting techniques and equipment, but the vast majority of all military jumps are static-line operations.

The universal static line (USL) used with the T10D parachute is a fifteen-foot length of bright yellow nylon tubing. A five-foot extension is added when jumping from certain aircraft, such as the C-17A Globemaster III. The exposed end of the static line has a hook, which is attached to an anchor cable inside the aircraft prior to jumping. The other end of the static line is attached to the deployment bag, which is inside the parachute pack tray on the jumper's back. The pack is closed with break tape, a cord designed to snap under stress.

A BAC student exits a Lockheed C-141 over Fryar Drop Zone. The static line is stowed on the parachute pack by retainer bands, which keeps the static line from becoming fouled or tangled before exiting the aircraft. As the jumper leaves the door, the static line is pulled out of the retainer bands and fully extends, pulling the deployment bag from the parachute pack.

When the jumper exits the aircraft, the static line extends to its full length and pulls the deployment bag from the jumper's pack. The canopy and suspension lines are folded inside the deployment bag, and the apex of the canopy is attached to the bag by break tape. The static line and deployment bag stay with the aircraft, while the jumper falls away from the aircraft. The parachute is packed in the deployment bag so that the suspension lines fully extend before the canopy is pulled out by the weight of the falling paratrooper.

After being fully pulled from the bag, the canopy starts to inflate with air. The top inflates first, creating a shape similar to a squid. If everything works as advertised, the canopy opens quickly, creating an abrupt deceleration known as "opening shock." The severity of the opening shock varies but can be mitigated by a proper exit from the aircraft and by the jumper maintaining a tight body position during opening.

After the entire stick has exited the aircraft, the jumpmaster (or safety, if the jumpmaster exited with the stick) will check for towed jumpers. Then, the deployment bags are pulled back into the aircraft by their attached static lines.

THE LONG WAIT FOR THE SHORT DROP

One common memory shared by most veterans, regardless of branch, about their time in military service is the "hurry up and wait" syndrome. This is when short bursts of intense, often frantic, activity are interrupted by prolonged periods of waiting for the next burst of activity. The student-jump experience at BAC is similar to riding the best rollercoaster at a big theme park. It is a very long wait for a very short, but thrilling, ride.

There are reasons that this process takes so long. First, the jumps are still taking place in an instructional atmosphere, and the students are learning as they go. As they gain experience, they will be able to execute the prejump procedures more quickly and with fewer errors. Second, there are many things that jumpers need to do, and do correctly, before walking across the tarmac and up the ramp of a C-130. There are sustained airborne training, jumpmaster briefings, parachute issue, equipment donning, and jumpmaster personnel inspections for safety. Also, some part of this is interrupted by a chow break. Third, weather and aircraft maintenance issues are beyond the control of anybody at McCarthy Hall. Finally, it is the unchanging nature of military service that moving hundreds of soldiers at a time is rarely a smooth operation. Roman centurions probably had a Latin phrase for hurry up and wait.

Although student-jump operations at BAC vary from class to class, we can outline what constitutes a "typical" prejump process. Some activities may occur in a different order, depending on operational needs. It all starts at least five to six hours prior to the final jump command, sometimes more. For instance, a jump scheduled for 1000 hours will require that students muster outside the barracks at 0330 for inspection and movement to Lawson Field, and arrive at McCarthy Hall by 0430 hours for the operations brief and sustained airborne training. Fatigue is a constant factor at BAC, which is another reason for multilayered safety checks. Training days that have two jump operations are brutally exhausting.

OPERATION BRIEFING

As soon as practical after the initial manifest call, the jumpmaster conducts a brief on the details of the operation. The brief should include the following:

- Drop zone

- Type of aircraft

- Chalk number(s)

- Type of parachute(s)

- Briefing on serials, container delivery system, heavy drop, and type of aircraft, if a part of a larger airborne operation

- Weather (time for go or no-go decision)

- Type of individual equipment and separate equipment with which troops will be jumping (CWIE, AIRPAC, DMJP, ALICE pack, SMJP, M1950 weapons case)

- Time and place of parachute issue

- Load time

- Station time

- Takeoff time

- Length of flight

- Time on target

- Direction of flight over DZ

- Drop altitude

- Predicted speed and direction of winds on the DZ

- Route checkpoints

- DZ assembly aids and area

- Parachute turn-in point(s)

(Above) A parachutist is at near full extension of the suspension lines as the canopy is pulled from the deployment bag. The apex of the canopy is attached to the deployment bag by break tape, which ensures that the parachute is fully extended before it starts to inflate. *Gregory Mast*

(Left) Deployment bags remain attached to the static line and are retrieved into the aircraft after each stick of jumpers.

(Next spread) Students are in McCarthy Hall, waiting for their ride to show up. Students may spend many hours waiting to board the jump aircraft during jump week, after they have donned their equipment and finished jumpmaster personnel inspections (JMPI). *Hans Halberstadt*

- Time and place of final manifest call

- Medical support plan

- Obstacles on or near the DZ

SUSTAINED AIRBORNE TRAINING

Following the operation briefing, sustained airborne training is conducted in the unit area or at the departure airfield. Sustained airborne training (SAT) is a required prejump activity for every U.S. Army parachute operation. The rationale for this is that jumpmasters in the real world outside the boundaries of Fort Benning may not know the proficiency of the jumpers that are his responsibility. The jumpmaster has a script that defines the minimum scope of the training, which he may administer up to forty-eight hours before jumping but not less than two hours before boarding the jump aircraft. Basic jump techniques are rehearsed so each parachutist can demonstrate proficiency. Jumpmasters, safeties, and key leaders will make on-the-spot corrections to any jumper not properly performing the required training. For BAC students, this is a condensed version of the training syllabus of the previous two weeks and takes about an hour and a half to complete.

Prejump training is performance oriented and is tailored to fit the mission. At the Basic Airborne Course, this training is conducted outside McCarthy Hall in an area specifically designated for this purpose. Once the students graduate and go to an airborne unit, the training may be conducted with field-expedient training apparatus, as necessary. Prior to beginning prejump training, jumpmaster personnel check ID cards, ID tags, and ballistic helmets for serviceability and proper routing of parachutist helmet retention strap.

Sustained airborne training is mandated in FM 3-21.220 and defined by unit standard operating procedures. Sustained airborne training consists of, at a minimum, PLFs and mock-door training, a review of the five points of performance, towed jumper procedures, collisions and entanglements, malfunctions, activation of the reserve, and emergency landings. Mock-door training will include rehearsal of every detail involved with the airborne operation, to include accidental activation of the reserve parachute on board the aircraft. Jumpers must make a minimum of two exits from the mock door. Jumpmasters conduct this training from standard scripts that are tailored to the mission. A sample script from the jumpmaster course follows:

"The first items I will cover are the points of performance. Your first point of performance is proper exit, check body position and count. Jumpers, hit it. Upon exiting the aircraft, snap into a good, tight body position. Keep your eyes open, chin on your chest, elbows tight into your sides, hands on the end of the reserve, with your fingers spread, right hand covering the ripcord grip. If jumping the MIRPS/SLCP, place your hands on the end of the reserve, with your fingers spread. Bend forward at the waist, keeping your feet and knees together, knees locked to the rear, and count to four thousand.

"At the end of your four thousand count, immediately go into your second point of performance, check canopy and gain canopy control. When jumping the T10-series parachute, reach up to the elbow-locked position and secure a set of risers in each hand, simultaneously, conduct a 360-degree check of your canopy. When jumping the MC1-1 series parachute, secure a toggle in each hand and pull them down to eye level, simultaneously conducting a 360-degree check of your canopy. If, during your second point of performance, you find that you have twists, reach up and grasp a set of risers with each hand, thumbs down, knuckles to the rear. Pull the risers apart and begin a vigorous bicycling motion. When the last twist comes out, immediately check canopy and gain canopy control.

"Your third point of performance is keep a sharp lookout during your entire descent. Remember the three rules of the air and repeat them after me: always look before you slip or turn, always slip or turn in the opposite direction to avoid collisions, and the lower jumper always has the right of way. Avoid fellow jumpers all the way to the ground, and maintain a twenty-five-foot separation when jumping the T10 series parachute and a fifty-foot separation when jumping the MC1-1 series parachute. Sometime during your third point of performance, release all appropriate equipment tie-downs.

"This brings you to your fourth point of performance, which is prepare to land. At one hundred to two hundred feet AGL, look below you to ensure there are no fellow jumpers, and lower your equipment. Regain canopy control. At approximately one hundred feet AGL, slip or turn into the wind and assume a landing attitude. When jumping the T10-

series parachute and the wind is blowing from your left, reach up on the left set of risers and pull them deep into your chest. If the wind is blowing from your front, reach up on the front set of risers and pull them deep into your chest. If the wind is blowing from your right, reach up on your right set of risers and pull them deep into your chest. If the wind is blowing from your rear, reach up on your rear set of risers and pull them deep into your chest. When jumping the MC1-1 series parachute and the wind is blowing from your left, pull your left toggle down to the elbow-locked position. When you are facing into the wind, let up slowly to prevent oscillation. If the wind is blowing from your right, pull your right toggle down to the elbow-locked position. When you are facing into the wind, let up slowly to prevent oscillation. If the wind is blowing from your rear, pull either toggle down to the elbow-locked position. When you are facing into the wind, let up slowly to prevent oscillation. If the wind is blowing from your front, make minor corrections to remain facing into the wind. Once you are facing into the wind, assume a landing attitude by keeping your feet and knees together, knees slightly bent, with your head and eyes on the horizon.

"When the balls of your feet make contact with the ground, you will go into your fifth point of performance, land. You will make a proper PLF by hitting all five points of contact. Touch them and repeat them after me: 1) balls of the feet, 2) calf, 3) thigh, 4) buttocks, 5) pull-up muscle. You will never attempt to make a stand-up landing.

"Remain on your back and activate one of your canopy-release assemblies using either the hand-to-shoulder method or the hand-assist method. To activate your canopy-release assembly using the hand-to-shoulder method, with either hand reach up and secure a safety clip and pull it out and down, exposing the cable loop. Insert the thumb from bottom to top through the cable loop, turn your head in the opposite direction, and pull out and down on the cable loop. To activate the canopy-release assembly using the hand-assist method, with either hand reach up and secure a safety clip and pull it out and down exposing the cable loop. Insert the thumb from bottom to top. Re-enforce that hand with the other hand, turn your head in the opposite direction, and pull out and down

on the cable loop. If your canopy fails to deflate, activate the other canopy-release assembly. Place your weapon into operation, and remain on your back to get out of the parachute harness.

"Recovery of equipment: Once out of the parachute harness, remove all air items from the parachute harness. Roll the aviator's kit bag two-thirds down and place the parachute harness inside the aviator's kit bag, smooth side facing up, leaving the waistband exposed. Remain on a knee and begin pulling the suspension and canopy to the aviator's kit bag, stuffing them into the aviator's kit bag as you go. Route the waistband through the bridal loop, leaving six to eight inches of the waistband exposed, then snap, do not zip, the aviator's kit bag. Secure the reserve parachute to the aviator's kit bag, place it over your head, conduct a 360-degree police of your area, and move to your assembly area.

"Towed jumper procedures: If you become a towed jumper and are being towed by your static line and are unconscious, you will be retrieved inside the aircraft. If you are conscious, maintain a good, tight body position with your right hand protecting your ripcord grip, and an attempt will be made to retrieve you inside the aircraft. If jumping the MIRPS/SLCP, place your left hand on the end of the reserve and with your right hand cover the ripcord protective flap, while resting the right forearm on the ripcord grip.

"As you near the jump door, do not reach for us, [but] continue to protect your ripcord grip. If you cannot be retrieved, you will be cut free. Once you feel yourself falling free from the aircraft, immediately activate your reserve parachute for a total malfunction.

"If you are being towed by your equipment, regardless of whether you are conscious or unconscious, we will cut or jog your equipment free, and your main parachute will deploy.

"Note: If you are being towed from a rotary-wing aircraft, maintain a good, tight body position and protect your ripcord grip. The aircraft will slowly descend to the DZ, come to a hover, and the jumpmaster will free you from the aircraft.

"The next item I will cover is malfunctions. There are two types of malfunctions, total and partial. A total malfunction provides no lift capability whatsoever; therefore, you must activate your reserve using the pull-drop method. While cigarette rolls and streamers are partial malfunctions, they provide no lift capability and you must activate your reserve using the pull-drop method.

"There are several types of partial malfunctions and actions for each. If you have broken suspension lines, blown sections, or gores, compare your rate of descent with fellow jumpers. If you are falling faster than fellow jumpers, activate your reserve for a partial malfunction. If you have a squid, semi-inversion, or a complete inversion with damage to the canopy or suspension lines, you must immediately activate your reserve for a partial malfunction. If you have a complete inversion with no damage to the canopy or suspension lines, do not activate your reserve parachute.

"The modified improved reserve parachute system (MIRPS): To activate the system, you will use the pull-drop method. Jumpers, hit it! Maintain a good, tight body position. Grasp the left carrying handle with your left hand; with your right hand grasp the ripcord grip. Pull out on the ripcord grip and drop it. Your reserve will activate. If your reserve does not activate, maintain a good, tight body position, and with your right hand form a knife-cutting edge and sweep the ripcord protector flap up and away allowing the deployment assistance device to properly deploy. To activate the T10 reserve for a total malfunction, use the pull-drop method. Jumpers, hit it! If you do not feel an opening shock at the end of your count, maintain a good, tight body position. With your left hand, grasp the left carrying handle; with your right hand, grasp the ripcord grip. Turn your head to the left or right; pull the ripcord grip, and drop it. Your reserve will activate. To activate the T10 reserve for a partial malfunction, use the down-and-away method. Check canopy and gain canopy control. Jumpers, hit it! Snap back into a good, tight body position. With the left hand, cover the ripcord protector flap, and with the right hand, grasp the ripcord grip. Apply inward pressure with the left hand, and with the right hand pull the ripcord grip and drop it. Form a knife-cutting edge with the right hand, and insert it into the upper right-hand corner of the reserve. Grasp as much canopy (and suspension lines) as possible, and pull it out and up over either shoulder and throw it down and away in the direction you are spinning. If the canopy fails to inflate, pull it back into your body and throw it down and away in the opposite direction. Once your reserve activates, with each hand form a fist, thumbs exposed, and with a sweeping motion, clear all of the suspension lines from the pack assembly, ensuring they are deployed.

"Note: if you have to activate the reserve for a partial malfunction, any attempt to control either canopy will be useless, as one canopy will act as a brake for the other.

"The next items I will cover are collisions and entanglements. Jumpers, hit it. Check canopy and gain canopy control. If you see another jumper approaching, immediately attempt to slip or turn away. If you cannot avoid the collision, assume a spread-eagle body position and attempt to bounce off the jumper's canopy and suspension lines and immediately slip or turn away. If you pass through the suspension lines, snap into a modified position of attention. With your right hand, protect your ripcord grip, and with your left hand, attempt to weave your way out of the suspension lines the same way you entered, and then slip or turn away.

"If you become entangled and are jumping the T10-series parachute, the higher jumper will climb down to the lower jumper using the hand-under-hand method. Once both jumpers are even, you will face each other and grasp each other's left main lift web with your left hand. Both jumpers will discuss which PLF to execute. Both jumpers will conduct the same PLF. Neither jumper will execute a front PLF. Both jumpers will continue to observe their canopies. If one canopy collapses, neither jumper will activate their reserve, as one T10 series parachute can safely deliver two combat-equipped jumpers to the ground. If both canopies collapse, the jumpers will pull toward each other to create a clear path for the activation of their reserve parachutes and activate their reserves using the pull-drop method.

"If you are jumping the MC1-1 series parachute, both jumpers will remain where they are, obtain a clear path, and immediately activate their reserve parachutes using the pull-drop method.

"The next items I will cover are emergency landings. The first emergency landing I will cover is the tree landing. If you are drifting toward the trees, immediately slip or turn away. If you cannot avoid the trees and have lowered your equipment, look below you to ensure there are no fellow jumpers, and jettison your equipment, making a mental note of where it lands. If you have not lowered your equipment, keep it on you to provide extra protection while passing through the trees. At approximately one hundred feet AGL, assume a landing attitude by keeping your feet and knees together, knees slightly bent, with your head and eyes on the horizon. When the balls of your feet make contact with the trees, rotate your hands in front of your face with your elbows high. Be prepared to execute a PLF if you pass through the trees.

"If you get hung up in the trees, keep your ballistic helmet on and lower and jettison all unneeded equipment. Activate the chest-strap ejector snap and activate the quick release in your waistband. Place your left hand over the ripcord protector flap and apply pressure. Grasp the ripcord grip with your right hand, then pull it and drop it. Control the activation of the reserve parachute toward the ground, ensuring that all suspension lines are completely deployed. Disconnect the left connector snap and rotate the reserve to the right. Grasp the main lift web with either hand below the canopy- release assembly, and with the other hand activate the leg-strap ejector snaps and climb down the outside of the reserve. Remember, when in doubt, stay where you are and wait for assistance.

"The next emergency landing I will cover is the wire landing. If you are drifting toward wires, immediately slip or turn away. If you cannot avoid the wires, look below you to ensure there are no fellow jumpers, and lower and jettison your equipment, making a mental note of where it lands. Assume a landing attitude by placing your hands, fingers, and thumbs extended and joined high on the inside of the front set of risers, with the elbows locked. Place your chin on your chest, keep your feet and knees together, and exaggerate the bend in your knees. When the balls of your feet make contact with the wires, begin a vigorous rocking motion in an attempt to pass all the way through the wires. Be prepared to execute a PLF if you pass all the way through the wires. If you get hung up in the wires, stay where you are and wait for assistance.

"The last emergency landing I will cover is the water landing. The water landing is the most

dangerous emergency landing, because it takes the most time to prepare for. If you are drifting toward a body of water, immediately slip or turn away. If you cannot avoid the water, look below you to ensure there are no fellow jumpers, and lower, do not jettison, your equipment. Next, jettison your ballistic helmet. Activate the quick release in your waistband, disconnect the left connector snap, and rotate the reserve to the right. Seat yourself well into the saddle, and activate the chest-strap ejector snap. Regain canopy control. Prior to entering the water, assume a landing attitude by keeping your feet and knees together, knees slightly bent, and place your hands on the leg-strap ejector snaps. When the balls of your feet make contact with the water, activate the leg-strap ejector snaps, arch your back, throw your arms above your head, and slide out of the parachute harness. Swim upwind or upstream away from the canopy. Be prepared to execute a PLF if the water is shallow. If the canopy comes down on top of you, locate a radial tape, follow it to the skirt of the canopy, and swim upstream or upwind away from the canopy.

"The next items I will discuss are mission-oriented items. Because intentional water landings, night operations, and operations under AWADS [adverse weather aerial delivery system] conditions require additional considerations, you must be prepared to brief them to your jumpers.

"Note: if you are jumping the B7 life preserver, activate it in the air. Lower but do not jettison combat equipment.

"Night jumps: when conducting night jumps, be sure to give your canopy an extra look, and maintain noise and light discipline all the way to the ground.

"AWADS: when jumping under adverse weather aerial delivery system (AWADS) conditions, do not lower your equipment until you have passed through the clouds. Do not slip or turn unless you have to avoid a collision. If you have any type of malfunction, you must immediately activate your reserve using the pull-drop method, because you cannot compare your rate of descent with fellow jumpers. Ensure you recheck your canopy once you pass through the clouds.

"PLFs: we will now move to the PLF platform and conduct one satisfactory PLF in each of the four directions ensuring you conduct a proper PLF."

JUMPMASTER PERSONNEL INSPECTIONS

After students draw their parachutes from the rigging shed, they go to McCarthy Hall to don the equipment. When they are finished, the Black Hats conduct rigorous and thorough safety checks called jumpmaster personnel inspections (JMPI). The JMPI is a complete and systematic inspection of every piece of equipment on the jumper to ensure that each item is serviceable and correctly assembled. This is a hands-on inspection in which the Black Hat touches every piece of equipment. The principle is to touch and visually inspect each item to make sure that it is not twisted, cut, frayed, or misrouted. When tracing metal items, the jumpmaster inspects for sharp edges and proper assembly. When performing the JMPI, the jumpmaster starts at the point of attachment to the parachute harness and completely inspects that item before proceeding with the remainder of the inspection sequence. As with everything else at BAC, this inspection is conducted exactly as scripted, because deviation from the script could allow a jumper to board the aircraft in an unsafe condition.

The sequence is top to bottom on the front of the jumper, then top to bottom on the back. There are highly specific standards for each item inspected. For instance, here is an example of inspection script for the ballistic helmet:

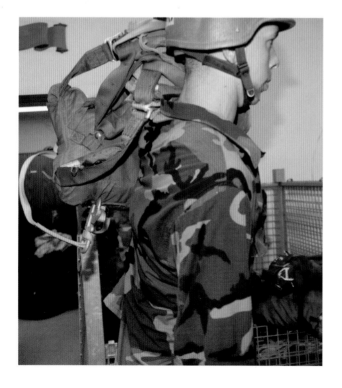

"The jumpmaster will move to his jumper and issue the command, 'Open your ripcord protector flap.' The jumpmaster will place both hands on the extreme right-hand side; fingers and thumb extended and joined, fingers pointed skyward, palms facing the jumper. The left hand is the control hand. The right hand is the working hand. With the working hand, trace across the rim of the ballistic helmet to the opposite side, inspecting for any sharp or protruding edges that may damage or cut the jumper's static line upon exiting the aircraft. Once the hands are parallel, insert the thumb of each hand under the rim of the ballistic helmet and feel for the locking nut to ensure that it is present and secured. Tilt the jumper's head to the rear and look at the headband. Ensure the smooth leather portion of the headband is toward the jumper's head and that the securing tabs are present and secure. Place the right index finger on the pull-the-dot fastener with tab. Insure that it is a serviceable pull-the-dot fastener with tab, in that it has four plies of nylon in the tab portion, three of which must run through the snap portion, and the snap portion is secured. Bypass the pull-the-dot fastener with tab and trace down to the point of attachment for the chinstrap. Insure the chinstrap is properly routed through the adjusting buckle and that the parachutist retention strap is routed around the chinstrap, under the adjusting buckle, and the pile portion of the parachutist retention strap is away from the jumper's face. Trace the long, continuous portion of the chinstrap under the jumper's chin to its point of attachment on the opposite side, and conduct the same inspection. Now, place the index finger of the right hand on the inside of the nylon portion of the adjusting buckle and trace it up until you make skin-to-skin contact with the left thumb still in place on the locking nut. Trace the short sewn portion chinstrap across the front of the jumper's chin, and drop both hands.

(Left) After getting their reserve parachute, students draw their main parachute. Students assist the cadre during this exercise by issuing jump gear. *Gregory Mast*

After "ballistic helmet (front)," the subsequent items in a Hollywood jump safety checklist are as follows:

- Canopy-release assemblies

- Chest strap

- Waist band

- Reserve

- Leg straps

- Universal static line

- Pack-opening loop, pack-closing loops, pack-closing tie

- Ballistic helmet (rear)

- Riser assemblies

- Pack tray

- Diagonal back straps

- Horizontal back straps

- Saddle

The T10D parachute ready to go. Visible in this photograph are the diagonal back straps of the troop parachute harness, which are adjusted to fit the jumper. *Gregory Mast*

Before donning the parachute, students put on the parachutist ankle brace (PAB). The PAB stabilizes the jumper's ankle during PLFs and reduces the potential for ankle injury. The PAB, which is worn outside the combat boot, consists of sidewalls that extend vertically to encircle the ankle and the lower leg. *Gregory Mast*

A kit bag is secured underneath the leg straps of the troop parachute harness. The kit bag is used to stow the parachute and harness after the parachutist has landed on the drop zone. *Gregory Mast*

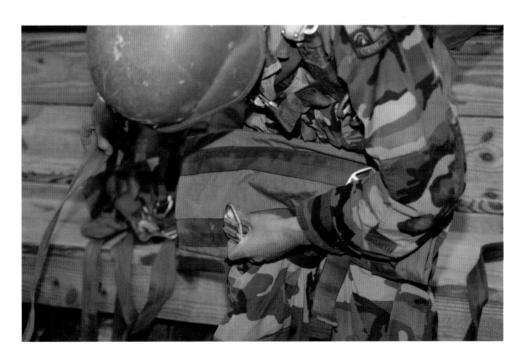

(Above) After the chest strap of the troop parachute harness is secured, the leg straps are attached. *Gregory Mast*

(Opposite bottom) Lawson Army Air Field, located on the Fort Benning Military Reservation, is where BAC students conduct prejump training, are issued jump equipment, and board jump aircraft. Here, students move from McCarthy Hall to the rigging shed to draw parachutes. *Gregory Mast*

In the rigging shed, students are issued reserve parachutes first.
Gregory Mast

Some things never change about military service. During the hectic
schedule of jump school, students take meal breaks whenever possible.
During jump week, students often eat breakfast in the predawn
darkness after completing prejump training. *Gregory Mast*

(Above) Students use the buddy system when donning parachutes. Using this system to properly don and adjust the troop parachute harness provides an additional safety check, prevents delays during JM inspection, and provides minimum discomfort to the parachutist while aboard the aircraft or when receiving the opening shock of the parachute. The buddy system provides the best combination of speed and accuracy for parachutists to adjust and check each other's parachutes. *Gregory Mast*

(Right) Students check one another's equipment during the donning process. Multiple layers of equipment checks and safety inspections are critical, because parachuting remains an inherently hazardous activity. A simple mistake made by a fatigued parachutist could have life-or-death implications on the drop zone. *Gregory Mast*

(Above) Jumpmaster personnel inspections (JMPI) are formal, hands-on safety inspections conducted by the jumpmaster. The process starts when the jumpmaster instructs the student to place his hands on his helmet. The JMPI is a top-to-bottom, back-to-front process that follows a standard script, ensuring that every critical piece of equipment is inspected before the student boards the jump aircraft. *Hans Halberstadt*

(Below) Jumpmasters look at and touch every piece of equipment they inspect during JMPI. They follow a meticulous script that specifically details how each item will be inspected. Here the jumpmaster is inspecting the waistband, as directed by the JMPI script: "Insert the left hand, fingers and thumb extended and joined fingers pointed skyward, palm facing the jumpmaster, from the bottom to the top behind the waistband next to where it is sewn into the pack tray. Look at the waistband where it is sewn into the pack tray, and insure that at least 50 percent of one row of stitching is present. Trace the waistband forward to insure that it is not twisted, cut, frayed, or been misrouted behind the horizontal back strap. Trace the waistband forward until the left hand makes contact with the right D-ring. Look at the waistband to insure that it is routed over the right main lift web and under the right D-ring." *Hans Halberstadt*

After the JMPI is complete, the long wait begins. Students are seated on long wooden benches, constructed to accommodate a jumper wearing a parachute in a reasonable state of comfort for about twenty minutes or until your butt falls asleep, whichever comes first. Soon, the students are confronted by the twin enemies of military instruction: boredom and fatigue. An hour spent waiting in McCarthy Hall can seem to be an eternity. Some students try to snatch a few minutes of sleep. Others talk and joke as soldiers have always done, but most sit in silent thought about the upcoming jump. McCarthy Hall has two temperatures, too hot and too cold, but it is still better than waiting on the tarmac, in the sun or the rain.

A jumpmaster checks the M1950 weapons case during JMPI. From the script, "With the right index finger, finger the opening gate one time to insure that it is properly attached to the left D-ring, it has spring tension, and it has not been safetied. With the heel of the right hand, press up on the activating arm of the quick-release snap to insure that it is seated between the ball detents. With the index finger of the right hand, trace down until contact is made with the V-ring. Insure the quick-release link is routed through the V-ring, and the quick-release link is secured by the rotating claw." *Hans Halberstadt*

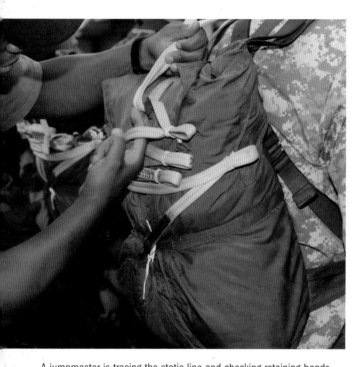

A jumpmaster is tracing the static line and checking retaining bands during JMPI. From the script, "Trace the first strand of universal static line over to the second stow to insure that it is free of all cuts, frays, and burns. Once contact is made with the second stow, pinch it off with the index finger and thumb of the working hand, pull it one to two inches toward the center of the pack tray, and conduct the same inspection." *Gregory Mast*

(Opposite) After JMPI and hit-it drills are complete, students wait in McCarthy Hall on specially constructed benches designed to accommodate a soldier wearing a parachute. *Hans Halberstadt*

Students practice the hit-it drill after JMPI. In this drill, the students rehearse the points of performance and emergency actions they may have to take in the event of a parachute malfunction. *Gregory Mast*

Students at BAC will spend hours sitting on the benches in McCarthy Hall during jump week. Bad weather or aircraft maintenance issues will occasionally create delays as well. *Hans Halberstadt*

Some students manage to catch a few minutes' sleep while waiting for their jump aircraft to arrive. *Hans Halberstadt*

This student's helmet indicates that he is a "chalk leader" (CL). A "chalk" is one planeload of paratroopers, which may consist of several "sticks," or groups of paratroopers who exit the aircraft together during a single pass over the drop zone. The student chalk leader has several tasks, not the least of which is making sure all the jumpers on his aircraft make it on board. *Hans Halberstadt*

The Lockheed C-130 Hercules is the most commonly used jump aircraft at BAC and is one of the most versatile military aircraft in history. The C-130 has been in continuous production since 1954, and more than 2,260 Hercules have been built for sixty-seven countries. *Gregory Mast*

After a long wait, students scramble out of McCarthy Hall and onto the tarmac to board their jump aircraft. *Hans Halberstadt*

Students follow their student chalk leader out of McCarthy Hall. The chalk leader will lead the chalk across the tarmac and work with the jumpmaster and air crew to ensure that all jumpers are accounted for prior to the aircraft taking off. *Gregory Mast*

The walk to the aircraft can seem to be much longer than it really is under a hot Georgia sun. This photograph provides a good illustration of the M1950 weapons case and the harness, single-point release (HSPR) leg straps that stabilize the ALICE pack rigged for jump operations. *Gregory Mast*

The sound of turboprop engines and the smell of their exhaust in the prop blast greet the jumpers as they approach their ride to the drop zone. Students who are film buffs may recognize this airfield from the 1967 film *The Green Berets*. Lawson Army Airfield doubled for Da Nang in that Vietnam war film starring John Wayne. *Gregory Mast*

Black Hats control student movement from McCarthy Hall to the aircraft. A live tarmac can be a hazardous area, both for the soldiers during troop movement and for the aircraft. *Gregory Mast*

Walking is a chore when combat equipment is rigged for parachute operations. This photograph provides a good illustration of the harness, single-point release (HSPR) that attaches the ALICE pack to the troop parachute harness. Note the white release handle, located at the top center of the ALICE pack. When it is pulled, the pack detaches from the harness and drops to the end of the lowering line. *Hans Halberstadt*

THE PERFECTLY GOOD AIRPLANE

Students at BAC will jump from either a C-130 Hercules or a C-17A Globemaster III, provided courtesy of the U.S. Air Force. The air force also uses student-jump operations as refresher training on parachute operations for the pilots and air crews. Aircraft are tasked from active duty and reserve units and come in a variety of configurations and models. The C-130 is the most common aircraft for student-jump operations and is one of the most versatile military aircraft in history. It has been in constant production for nearly fifty years and has nearly run through the entire alphabet in naming variants and models of this aircraft. Many of the Hercules aircraft are older than the students jumping out of them.

Students board the aircraft by sticks. It can be a long walk across the tarmac, especially on a hot day when loaded down with combat equipment. A Black Hat conducts a final, quick inspection of equipment before the students walk up the rear ramp of the airplane. Students have rehearsed every action they will take up until this point, practiced every move, recited the four thousand count like a mantra, and exercised to the point of exhaustion, all for this moment when they board the jump aircraft. The next time their feet touch ground will be on the drop zone.

NEXT STOP, ALABAMA

Fryar Drop Zone is located about six miles southeast of Lawson Field, on the Alabama side of Fort Benning. Flying time depends on the weather, the number of jumpers, and whether the pilot is trying to rack up his frequent-flier miles. For many students, their first jump at BAC may be their first ride on a military cargo aircraft. Nervous fliers may not find the ride entertaining, but for most jumpers the ride is an adventure and certainly more enjoyable than economy-class travel on commercial airlines. After the aircraft takes off, it will usually take a route that allows it to approach the drop zone from the southwest, a roundabout plan that ensures that the first jumper in the stick will spend at least half an hour in the airplane.

Each airplane will make one pass over the drop zone before students jump. During this pass, at least two "wind jumpers" will exit; these are parachutists whose falls the jumpmaster will observe in order to estimate the wind situation on the drop zone and make adjustments accordingly. At BAC these wind-test dummies are usually cadre

from the 507th or other parachutists who need a pay jump. The number of passes over the drop zone will be determined by the number of parachutists on the aircraft and the types of exits. Single-door, individual exits will require more passes than mass exits using both doors.

After the first pass over the drop zone, the jumpmaster will give the ten-minute time warning to the stick. Now the game starts for real. Many students worry that they will freeze in the door when their turn comes. Some do, most don't. The nature of the training at BAC makes the execution of jump command instinctive, and many students don't realize that they had second thoughts about jumping until they are already under canopy.

It is on the first jump that the students understand why they rehearsed the jump commands and signals so often on the ground. It is very noisy on board a jump aircraft, and only the first few jumpers in the stick can actually hear the jumpmaster's shouted commands. The noise, combined with an inattentive or distracted jumper, can lead to confusion if actions on board the aircraft are not thoroughly rehearsed before boarding. It bears repeating often that parachute operations are inherently dangerous, and confusion on board the jump aircraft can create a situation that may result in serious injury or death. To avoid this confusion, every jumper repeats every warning and every command, just as they rehearsed it on the ground. Although it is unlikely to happen at BAC, occasionally a sleeping jumper must be awakened by his buddy.

The air force flight crew inspects their temporary cargo destined for Fryar Drop Zone. The U.S. Air Force uses student jumps at Fort Benning to refresh their air crews in airborne operational procedures. Some of the air crews are jump qualified, but a good number openly wonder at the sanity of anyone who would leave an aircraft in flight that was not engulfed in flames. *Gregory Mast*

The chalk loads the aircraft over the aft cargo ramp. The ramp can be used for parachute operations. However, at BAC all students will exit the aircraft from the troop doors located just aft of the wheel wells. *Hans Halberstadt*

Jumpmasters and assistant jumpmasters conduct one final safety inspection before students board the aircraft. The number of safety checks and equipment inspections may seem excessive to someone who is not familiar with military operations, but one cardinal operational rule is that nothing is foolproof. If something can be broken, damaged, misrouted, mangled, unsecured, misconnected, maladjusted, or simply forgotten, however improbable, a soldier will find a way to do it. *Hans Halberstadt*

Economy-class travel on a Lockheed C-130. This photograph was taken near the port-side troop door, looking forward toward the cockpit. Note that the jumpers are protecting the ripcord handles of their reserve parachutes, to prevent accidental deployment. *Hans Halberstadt*

Jumpmasters don their BA18 parachutes after the plane has been loaded. The USAF emergency parachute BA18, back automatic parachute, is used by nonjumping jumpmasters and safety personnel onboard USAF aircraft. *Gregory Mast*

Flight crew are conducting preflight inspection of the jump aircraft. Contrary to what many paratroopers think, the first step in this inspection is not "Count the engines." *Gregory Mast*

OUT THE DOOR

For many students, the first time out the door is a memorable experience that will stay with them for life. Even veteran paratroopers with hundreds of jumps can still remember the first time they stepped out of an aircraft in flight. Time can have an elastic quality in these circumstances. The moments following the ten-minute warning can pass in the blink of an eye, and the four thousand count can feel like forever, even when shouted so quickly it sounds like one long word.

"One thousand," and you take a vigorous step up and out of the airplane into the slipstream, just like the thirty-four-foot tower, feeling the prop blast slap your body, looking down over your reserve at your boots.

"Two thousand"—*where the hell is that parachute? What's taking so long? Craaaap, I should have had a better body position.*

"Three thousand." *Okay, I think that is a tug. Where the hell is that parachute? Hey, I can see a long way from up here. His parachute is open; where the hell is mine?*

"Four thousand." *Okay, there it goes. Crap, this harness is tight. What took so long? Hey, this thing works!*

After opening shock, there is a surge of exhilaration, a thrilling moment of hanging under an open canopy a thousand feet above the ground with your classmates. Then, students are brought back to reality by "the voice of God." A powerful public address system is set up on the drop zone below. Students are collectively advised on the points of performance ("Check canopy! Check canopy!") and given individual instruction as they near the ground ("Jumper two-five-six, feet and knees together, don't look at the ground, dummy!").

The ground comes up quickly, with most students taking about ninety seconds or so to make the descent to the drop zone. Black Hats are stationed at points across the DZ to provide coaching and assistance as needed. Jumpers ignore the blunt advice of the Black Hats at their own peril. Some students learn quickly, some never at all, but most students need several jumps before they learn to handle their canopy, land into the wind, and execute a passable parachute landing fall.

After landing, students are expected to quickly recover their air equipment and head for the assembly point near the observation bleachers. It is about a half a mile from the center of the drop zone, but it seems much farther under the hot, Southern sun. At the assembly point, the students will turn in their parachutes, report to the accountability NCO, and wait for their sticks to muster.

A jumpmaster (JM) is conducting an initial outside air safety check before starting the jump-command sequence. The JM must make outside air-safety checks to ensure there are no unsafe conditions outside the aircraft: that is, aircraft in the formation to the rear that are below drop altitude, or other low-flying aircraft. From the same rest position, the JM leans far enough outside the aircraft to make a proper air-safety check and visually checks the direction of flight and all around the outside of the aircraft. The JM continues observing outside the aircraft and spotting for checkpoints en route to the DZ. *BAC cadre*

A jumpmaster is waiting to give the "Go" command to the first jumper in the stick. He is watching the drop zone below, waiting for the release point. *BAC cadre*

Students are exiting the starboard-side troop door over Fryar Drop Zone. Note the assistant jumpmaster in the foreground acting as a safety. The jumpers hand the safety their static lines before exiting in order to reduce the possibility of a jumper becoming entangled in a static line. *BAC cadre*

Students exit the port-side troop door and begin their four thousand count over Fryar Drop Zone. *BAC cadre*

The first jumper in the stick has just exited the port-side door. The remaining jumpers in the stick are quickly shuffling to the door. *BAC cadre*

Students conduct a mass exit over Fryar Drop Zone. These photos provide an illustration of the alternate door exit procedure for training (ADEPT) method of mass exits. In the ADEPT method, jumpmasters stagger the exits so that two jumpers do not leave from both troop doors at the same time. This reduces the possibility of a collision and entanglement outside the aircraft before the parachutes have been deployed. These photos also show many details of static-line parachuting and the canopy-deployment sequence. Several jumpers can be seen with deployment bags pulled from their parachute packs by the static line, at full extension and with canopies being pulled from the deployment bags. Note that when a canopy inflates, or "catches air," it inflates from the top down, making a characteristic squid shape. *Gregory Mast*

Students descend under a canopy during a Hollywood jump, in which the parachutist is not carrying combat equipment.

(Above left and right) The moment of impact.

(Right) Fryar Drop Zone, outlined in red, as seen from ten thousand feet above ground level. Basic Airborne Course students will not get this panoramic view, because their jumps are conducted from 1,250 feet above ground level. Fryar Drop Zone measures 2,500 meters north to south, and 1,500 meters east to west.

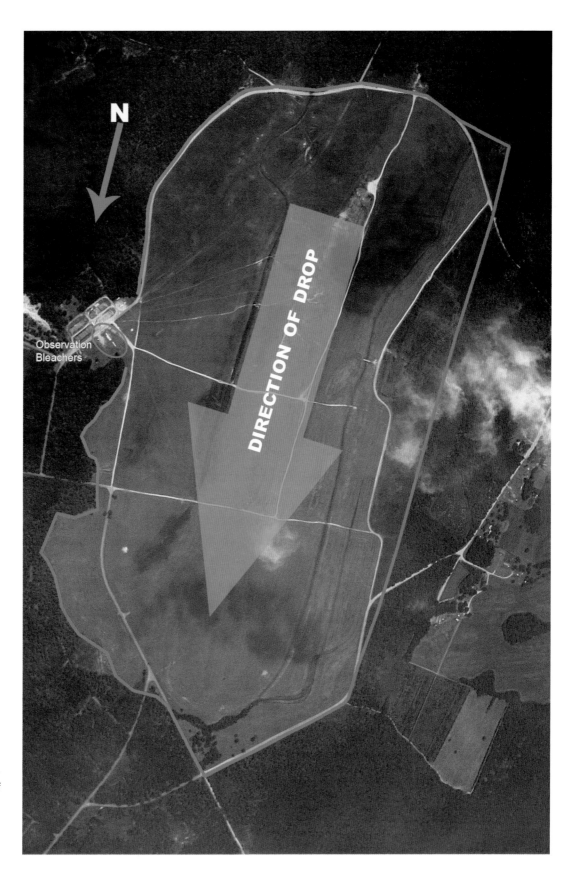

N

DIRECTION OF DROP

Observation Bleachers

(Left) Students head for the assembly point on the eastern edge of the DZ, about a half-mile walk across open terrain. *Gregory Mast*

117

Students who are the children or grandchildren of paratroopers are called into a special formation, where a jump-qualified parent or grandparent awards them their wings. This tradition dates back to the 1950s. *Hans Halberstadt*

THREE DAYS OF INSTRUCTION

"I went through the school during January of 1991. It was an unusual class because the weather was so bad that our jump week turned into two. We had rain and snow that prevented us from getting all five jumps in the normal schedule. In fact, we had to do two jumps on the second Saturday, and it wasn't until mid-February till we finally got done. The ground war [Operation Desert Storm] was just getting ready to launch about this time, and many of my class deployed soon after graduation.

"There is a saying that the Basic Airborne Course is three days of training packed into three weeks of instruction, and that is essentially true. Although the course was pretty physical, and I had problems with shin splints, it wasn't really that bad."

—Capt. Eric Graves, USAF (Ret.)

GRADUATION

Graduation ceremonies are usually held at the Airborne Walk on Eubanks Field. However, if weather or some other reason delays the scheduled jumps, graduation may be conducted on Fryar Drop Zone after the last jump. It is a short ceremony, although some of the guest speakers can make it seem much lengthier than it really is. Weather permitting, a demonstration team, like the Silver Wings, will make a freefall jump prior to the start of ceremonies. Honor graduates receive awards named after the first enlisted and commissioned paratroopers in the U.S. Army, recognizing the history and tradition of the Basic Airborne Course at Fort Benning.

Guests and family members are welcome to participate in awarding jump wings. Parents and grandparents who were paratroopers are allowed to pin wings on the newest paratrooper in their family first, and then everyone else is invited to do the same.

118

This navy petty officer is a hospital corpsman, or "Doc" as he is called by the marines that he supports. In addition to his new jump wings, he is also wearing the gold combatant diver badge. *Gregory Mast*

The practice of giving a new paratrooper "blood wings" is strictly prohibited by Department of Defense policy, as established by SECDEF Memo of 28 August 1997 (NOTAL). This is an old custom in which the jump wings would be pounded into the chest of the new paratrooper until the two retaining posts pierced and bloodied the skin under his uniform. Do not even think of doing this at the graduation ceremonies or anywhere on Fort Benning.

Out-processing will occupy the rest of your last day at BAC. You will want to make sure that every administrative detail is correct before you depart Fort Benning and take some well-earned leave. Administrative errors are much easier to prevent than they are to correct, as many an old-timer will tell you, so do not forget to get the proper endorsements on your orders in your haste to get out of Columbus.

THE ONE-EYED BLACK HAT

"One of my recollections was of a Black Hat instructor who only had one eye. He had lost the other during a training accident but was permitted to stay in the army and teach at the Basic Airborne Course. He was one of our jumpmasters and impressed us all with a story of having his glass eye popped out by the slipstream during one jump."

—Capt. Eric Graves, USAF (Ret.)

SIX

A navy SEAL tries to steer clear of his comrades as he parachutes into the Gulf of Mexico after jumping out of a U.S. Air Force MC-130E Combat Talon I on December 2, 2005. *Department of Defense photo by Senior Airman Andy M. Kin, U.S. Air Force*

Life After the Basic Airborne Course: Go

Soldiers of the 82nd Airborne Division execute a night jump with combat equipment somewhere over Fort Bragg. They are waiting for the "Stand by" command on board a Boeing C-17A Globemaster III.

For some graduates of the Basic Airborne Course, their last jump at Fort Benning will be the last jump of their military career. Most graduates, however, use their airborne qualification as an admission ticket to interesting and exciting assignments. A complete description of the opportunities available after jump school would take an entire book of its own. However, we can briefly outline a short, and incomplete, list of some of the challenges available to the newly minted paratrooper.

U.S. ARMY AIRBORNE DIVISIONS AND BRIGADES

The XVIII Airborne Corps is the army's largest warfighting organization and is the only airborne corps in the defense establishment of the United States. The XVIII Airborne Corps has control over approximately 88,000 soldiers. In the context of this book, the 82nd Airborne Division, located at Fort Bragg, North Carolina, and the 101st Airborne Division (Air Assault), located at Fort Campbell, Kentucky, are of particular interest. The U.S. Army's other large airborne formation is the 173rd Airborne Brigade, located at Caserma Ederle, Italy, and is assigned to Southern European Task Force (SETAF), United States Army Europe (USAREUR).

Airborne qualification is not an absolute necessity in order to be assigned to these conventional airborne units. On balance, however, life is much better in these outfits if you have jump wings.

According to GlobalSecurity.org, "The 82nd Airborne Division at Fort Bragg, North Carolina, provides the ability to begin executing a strategic airborne forcible entry into any area of the world within eighteen hours of notification. Their primary mission is airfield and seaport seizure. Once on the ground, they provide the secured terrain and facilities to rapidly receive additional combat forces. The division is the nation's strategic offensive force, maintaining the highest state of combat readiness.

"On any day, a third of the division is on mission cycle, ready to respond to any contingency. Another third is on a wartime training cycle, and the rest of the division is on support cycle. These support units prepare vehicles and equipment for deployment and support such other division and post activities.

"As the largest parachute force in the free world, the 82nd Airborne Division is trained to deploy anywhere, at any time, to fight upon arrival and to win. From cook to computer operator, from infantryman or engineer, every soldier in the 82nd is Airborne qualified. Almost every piece of divisional combat equipment can be dropped by parachute onto the field of battle."

According to GlobalSecurity.org, "The 101st Airborne Division (Air Assault) at Fort Campbell, Kentucky, provides forcible entry capability through heliborne air-assault operations. Capable of inserting a 4,000-soldier combined-arms task force 150 kilometers into enemy terrain in one lift, and possessing 281 helicopters, including three battalions of Apache attack helicopters, this division is the most versatile in the army. For

Paratroopers from the 82nd Airborne Division exit a C-17A over Fort Bragg. Note that the anti-inversion netting is clearly visible at the base of the opening canopies.

this reason, the 101st Airborne Division (Air Assault) is the division most in demand by combatant commanders.

"The 101st stands as the army's and world's only air assault division with unequaled strategic and tactical mobility. The 101st is unique in that it normally conducts operations 150 to 300 kilometers beyond the line of contact or forward-line-of-own-troops, requiring theater- and national-level intelligence support as a matter of course."

According to GlobalSecurity.org's mini-history of the 173rd Airborne Brigade, that unit "was reactivated on June 12, 2000, on Caserma Ederle in Vicenza, Italy, where it serves as European Command's only conventional airborne strategic response force for the European Theater. . . .

"On 26 March 2003 (not March 23, as sometimes reported), the 173rd Airborne Brigade conducted a jump into Northern Iraq in support of Operation Iraqi Freedom. . . . It does appear that it was the C-17's first-ever combat insertion of paratroopers. . . . Because they were in hostile air and because the drop zone was nestled in a valley, the C-17s had to go into an intense, steep dive from 30,000 feet to 600 feet. . . . The C-17s gave Washington the power to open and sustain a northern front when Turkey would not permit U.S. ground forces to use Turkish soil to invade Iraq. Fifteen C-17s airdropped 954 troops and equipment from the 173rd Airborne Brigade near Bashur on March 26. They were followed by an air-land insertion of forces."

A paratrooper from the 101st Airborne Division on duty in Iraq. The Airborne divisions of the U.S. Army have been committed to every theater in the Global War on Terror.

A squad of paratroopers from the 82nd Airborne Division take a break in Afghanistan.

THE 75TH RANGER REGIMENT

The 75th Ranger Regiment is headquartered at Fort Benning, Georgia. The regiment consists of four battalions. The 1st Battalion is located at Fort Stewart, Georgia; the 2nd Battalion at Fort Lewis, Washington; and the 3rd Battalion and the Ranger Training Brigade at Fort Benning, Georgia.

Airborne qualification and ranger qualification are both required for assignment to the 75th Ranger Regiment. Ranger training is among the most difficult in the U.S. armed forces. The Ranger Course is designed to further develop leaders who are physically and mentally tough and self-disciplined, and it challenges them to think, act, and react effectively in stress approaching that found in combat. The course is more than nine weeks in duration and divided into three phases: Benning Phase,

Fort Benning, Georgia; Mountain Phase, Dahlonega, Georgia; and Swamp Phase, Eglin Air Force Base, Florida. Success in the Ranger Course requires above-average intelligence, extraordinary physical endurance, and a supernaturally high threshold of pain.

According to GlobalSecurity.org, "The mission of the ranger regiment is to plan and conduct special military operations. These operations are conducted by specially trained, equipped, and organized forces against strategic or tactical targets in pursuit of national military, political, economic, or psychological objectives. They may support conventional military operations or they may be performed independently when conventional forces cannot be used.

"The flexibility of the ranger force requires it to perform under various command structures. The force

Members of A Company, 2nd Battalion, 3rd Special Forces Group, Fort Bragg, North Carolina, prepare to exit the ramp of a C-130 Hercules aircraft on a night jump, with oxygen and equipment, from 25,000 feet above Roosevelt Roads Naval Air Station, Puerto Rico.

U.S. Air Force members of the 41st Rescue Squadron, Moody Air Force Base, Georgia, jump out of a HC-130 troop door during a high altitude low opening (HALO) exercise during Exercise Desert Rescue VII near Naval Air Station Fallon, Nevada.

THE AIRBORNE OF THE FUTURE

"I am a big proponent of using parachute techniques to insert special operations forces covertly on clandestine operations. There are new systems that let a jumper 'fly' long distances after exiting the aircraft, and this is the sort of thing that offers tremendous utility when special forces personnel need to be inserted undetected into places they would not otherwise be able to get into.

"When the 82nd Airborne deployed before ground operations [for Operation Desert Storm] commenced in 1991, the common joke was that they would be not much more than a speed-bump for the Iraqi Army if it elected to take on American and coalition forces. An Airborne unit is always light and ill-equipped to take on a conventional force of the same approximate size. On the other hand, the rangers were able to jump into Panama and seize the airfields there during Operation Urgent Fury. And an airborne operation was the only practical way to put effective forces on the ground on Grenada during [Operation] Just Cause.

—Col. Gerald Schumacher, U.S. Army Special Forces (Ret.)

A U.S. Army jumpmaster makes a visual safety check at the open troop door of a C-141 Starlifter cargo transport aircraft in preparation for a parachute jump over a Fort Benning drop zone. Jumpmaster school is located at Fort Benning.

can work unilaterally under a corps, as a part of JSOTF [joint special operations task force], as an ARSOTF [army special operations task force], or as an army component in a JTF [joint task force]. Historically, it is common for the ranger force to conduct forced entry operations as part of a JSOTF, then become OPCON [under operational control] to a JTF to afford them the capability to conduct special operations and direct action missions.

"Special military operations conducted by the ranger regiment include strike operations, usually deep penetration and special light infantry operations. Strike operations include raids, interdiction, and recovery operations. Special light infantry operations include many of the light infantry missions assigned to airborne, air assault,

U.S. Army soldiers, 1st Battalion, 507th Parachute Infantry Regiment, Fort Benning, Georgia, re-enact the D-day parachute drop near Amfreville, France, as part of a sixteen-aircraft paratroop drop during the sixtieth anniversary of the Normandy Invasion.

Participating in Exercise Desert Rescue IX, a pararescueman assigned to the 66th Rescue Squadron, Nellis Air Force Base, Nevada, performs a HALO jump from a HC-130 Hercules transport aircraft of the 71st Rescue Squadron, Moody Air Force Base, Georgia.

or light infantry battalions and brigades. These operations are conducted in support of the air-land battle at all levels of intensity."

U.S. ARMY SPECIAL FORCES COMMAND (AIRBORNE): GREEN BERETS

The Green Berets, as the U.S. Army Special Forces are often called, are highly trained in unconventional warfare roles. Special forces units perform five doctrinal missions: foreign internal defense, unconventional warfare, special reconnaissance, direct action, and counter-terrorism. These missions make special forces unique in the U.S. military, because it is employed throughout the three stages of the operational continuum: peacetime, conflict, and war. The motto of the Green Beret is *De Oppresso Liber* (To Free the Oppressed).

Special Forces Command exercises command and control over five active component groups (1st, 3rd, 5th, 7th,

and 10th Special Forces Groups) and two Army National Guards groups (19th and 20th Special Forces Groups). Each special forces group is regionally oriented to support one of the war-fighting commanders in chief (CINCs).

Special forces soldiers routinely deploy in support of the CINCs of U.S. European Command, U.S. Atlantic Command, U.S. Pacific Command, U.S. Southern Command, and U.S. Central Command.

The mission of the U.S. Army Special Forces Command (Airborne) is to train, validate, and prepare special forces (SF) units to deploy and execute operational requirements for the U.S. military's warfighting commanders in chief throughout the world. Each group has three battalions, a group support company, and a headquarters company. The companies have six operational detachment alphas (ODA), or A-teams, assigned to them. The ODA is the heart and soul of SF operations.

(Below left and right) A combat control team (CCT) jumps from a C-130 for a HALO drop during the drop zone event of Rodeo '93.

(Above) U.S. Marines from 4th Force Reconnaissance Company, Kaneohe Bay, Hawaii, parachute out of a marine CH-53 Sea Stallion helicopter for day equipment jump training at Schofield Barracks in Oahu, Hawaii.

Special forces soldiers tend to be more intelligent than average and are often required to operate individually or in small groups in situations that are beyond the confines of traditional military operations. Unconventional warfare demands that soldiers have unconventional skills and abilities. Proficiency in foreign language skills is as important to a Green Beret as his personal weapon, and often more useful. The basic requirements for admission into the special forces training program are:

- Be a male, age twenty to thirty (special forces positions are not open to women)

- Be a U.S. citizen

- Be a high school graduate

- Achieve a general technical score of 110 or higher and a combat operation score of 98 on the Armed Services Vocational Aptitude Battery

- Qualify for a secret security clearance

- Qualify and volunteer for airborne training

- Take Defense Language Aptitude Battery or Defense Language Proficiency Test

- Achieve a minimum of 60 points on each event and overall minimum score of 229 on the Army Physical Fitness Test

According to GlobalSecurity.org, "The legendary green beret and the special forces tab are symbols of physical and mental excellence, courage, ingenuity, and just plain stubbornness. And the only place to get them is at the U.S. Army John F. Kennedy Special Warfare Center and School at Fort Bragg, North Carolina. At the heart of special forces training is the 1st Special Warfare Training Group, which conducts the Special Forces Assessment and Selection Course, Special Forces Qualification Course, and all advanced special forces skills training, such as language training and regional studies.

"The first step for a soldier wishing to become special forces qualified is Special Forces Assessment and Selection (SFAS); a twenty-four-day course designed to focus on student trainability and suitability in special forces. The SFAS cadre look at nearly 1,800 special forces volunteers each year to determine who is suitable for special forces training and to determine who may be unable to adapt to the special forces environment. Candidates attend SFAS at Camp MacKall, North Carolina, in a temporary duty (TDY) status. Candidates who enter this course find themselves under constant evaluation, starting with the day they in-process until the day they out-process.

"Teaching, coaching, training, and mentoring are important aspects of the program. Land navigation is used as a common medium to judge student trainability. A series of twelve attributes linked to success in the Special Forces Qualification Course (SFQC) form the basis for evaluating candidate suitability. These attributes include intelligence, physical fitness, motivation, trustworthiness, accountability, maturity, stability, judgment, decisiveness, teamwork, influence, and communications. Though land navigation is an important evaluation tool, other training events such as a one-mile obstacle course, runs, road marches, and rappelling are also used to evaluate students.

"A board of impartial senior officers and noncommissioned officers reviews the soldier's overall performance during the course. It makes the final determination as to whether the soldier is suitable for special forces training and identifies the specific special forces military occupational specialty for which he will be trained. After successfully completing the Special Forces Assessment and Selection Course, the soldier is then eligible to attend the Special Forces Qualification Course."

The special forces' training overview explains that "the Special Forces Qualification Course teaches and develops the skills necessary for effective utilization of the SF soldier. Duties in CMF (Career Management Field) 18 primarily involve participation in special operations-interrelated fields of unconventional warfare. These include foreign internal defense and direct-action missions as part of a small operations team or detachment. Duties at other levels involve command, control, and support functions. Frequently, duties require regional orientation to include foreign language training and in-country experience. SF places emphasis not only on unconventional tactics, but also on knowledge of nations in waterborne, desert, jungle, mountain, or arctic operations."

1ST SPECIAL FORCES OPERATIONAL DETACHMENT (AIRBORNE): DELTA FORCE

Little is known about Delta Force outside the tightly knit special operations community inside the U.S. armed forces. With the exception of a few high-profile missions, such as the infamous "Black Hawk Down" mission in Somalia, information available to the public is sketchy and largely anecdotal. This is the way the "operators" in Delta want to keep it.

The unit was secretly created in 1977 under the leadership of the legendary Col. Charles Beckwith and tasked with specialized missions relating to anti-terrorism. The unit's organization is somewhat similar to the special air service regiments of the British army. Delta is headquartered in a remote section of Fort Bragg, North Carolina, in a compound that is rumored to be the best training facility for special operations soldiers in the world.

The vast majority of Delta operators come from ranger battalions or special forces groups. However, candidates can be drawn from all branches of the army, including the Army Reserve and National Guard. According to SpecialOperations.com, "Those initially selected are usually chosen in one of three ways. The first of these is in response to advertisements posted at army bases across the country. The second method is by word of mouth, or personal recommendation from sources whose opinions are important to Delta screeners. Finally, on occasion the unit will require the skills of individuals who might not fall into one of the first two categories. If, in the instance that Delta's commanders

(Below) Wearing diving gear and armed with M4 carbines, members of a U.S. Navy Sea-Air-Land (SEAL) team emerge from the water during a press demonstration.

feel that an individual would make a valuable addition to the team (for example someone who speaks an obscure language or possesses hard-to-come-by technical skills), a representative from Delta will be dispatched specifically to interview that person."

ADVANCED PARACHUTE TRAINING SCHOOLS

The Basic Airborne Course at Fort Benning teaches the rudimentary or survival skills of military parachuting, which is basically how to not kill yourself or others around you during an airborne operation. As your career progresses and depending upon specialized assignments, you may require additional training in advanced parachute techniques and skills.

ADVANCED AIRBORNE SCHOOL, FORT BRAGG, NORTH CAROLINA

The mission of the Advanced Airborne School is to maintain the readiness of the XVIII Airborne Corps and the 82nd Airborne Division by preserving the ability to deploy anywhere in the world in eighteen hours by either an airborne or air-land assault. The school will train selected personnel in jumpmaster, air movement operations, and basic airborne techniques, as well as advising and assisting unit commanders in evaluation of jumpmasters and air movement operations officers and NCOs. Finally, the school will provide technical expertise to the XVIII Airborne Corps and 82nd Airborne Division Command Group pertaining to airborne operations.

JUMPMASTER SCHOOL, FORT BENNING, GEORGIA

The mission of the U.S. Army Jumpmaster School is to train personnel in the skills necessary to supervise a combat-equipped jump and the proper attaching, jumping, and releasing of combat and individual equipment while participating in an actual jump.

The course of instruction includes:

- Duties and responsibilities of the jumpmaster and safety

- Procedures for rigging individual equipment containers and door bundles

- Understanding and identifying personnel parachute components by their specific nomenclature and characteristics

- Procedures and standards required to conduct a jumpmaster personnel inspection

- The duties and responsibilities of the drop zone safety officer

- Presentation of the jumpmaster's briefings and prejump training

- The execution of the duties of a jumpmaster from a USAF aircraft during a day/night combat equipment jump

All students must be active U.S. Army or Reserve component officer or noncommissioned officer personnel in the rank of sergeant or higher. They must be qualified and current paratroopers, having jumped within 180 days of the class start date. Students must have a minimum of twelve static-line jumps from a high-performance aircraft (C-130, C-141, C-5, or C-17) and have been on jump status for a minimum of twelve months (need not be consecutive months). Students must be recommended by their battalion commander or officer in the rank of lieutenant colonel. Applicants must have a current and valid physical examination within five years of the class date, have passed the APFT within six months of entry to the course with a minimum score of 180 points (60 points in each event using the individual's age group), and meet the army height/weight standards IAW AR 600-9.

U.S. Marine Corps and Air Force officers and enlisted personnel, ranked sergeant and above, may attend if they have a minimum of twelve months on jump status and have completed twelve static-line jumps from a high-performance aircraft. Marine Corps corporals and USAF senior airmen (E-4) may also attend if they have twelve months on jump status and a minimum of fifteen static-line jumps.

PATHFINDER SCHOOL, FORT BENNING, GEORGIA

Pathfinders are trained in airborne, small-boat, vehicle, foot, and sometimes free-fall infiltration techniques. These small, four-man teams may be parachuted in up to seventy-two hours in advance of the main assault force. They provide drop zone/landing zone (DZ/LZ) surveys; site security; initial aircraft guidance; and marking and clearing of drop zones for follow-on forces. They are capable of engaging in demolition operations to clear DZ/LZs of obstacles. If equipped with laser-targeting designator (LTD), they may also designate targets of opportunity for air strikes. Pathfinders may be expected to coordinate aircraft movement, control parachute drops of personnel and equipment, conduct sling-load operations, and provide initial weather information to commanders.

The mission of the U.S. Army Pathfinder School is to provide a three-week course in which the student navigates dismounted; establishes and operates a day/night helicopter landing zone, a day/night computed air release point (CARP), ground-marked release system (GMRS), and army verbally initiated release system (VIRS) parachute DZ. Pathfinders are also trained to conduct sling-load operations and provide air-traffic control and navigational assistance to airborne operations. Students participate in a three-day field training exercise (FTX) as a member of a Pathfinder team.

MILITARY FREE FALL SCHOOL, FORT BRAGG, NORTH CAROLINA

Military Free Fall School, often called HALO School, is the pinnacle of military parachuting. During this four-week school, students learn one of the military's most demanding and potentially hazardous advanced skills, military free-fall (MFF). Parachute operations employing MFF are used to infiltrate enemy areas, often under the cover of darkness to avoid detection. Infiltration of oper-

A SEAL team member in full diving gear parachutes into the ocean during tactical warfare training.

Details of the MC4 parachute, the standard parachute used for military free-fall operations. *Gregory Mast*

ational elements, pilot teams, and personnel replacements is conducted under the cover of darkness, varying weather conditions, and terrain. Free-fall is a parachute maneuver in which the parachute is manually activated at the discretion of the jumper or automatically at a preset altitude.

The Military Free Fall School is taught by Company B, 2nd Battalion, 1st Special Warfare Training Group, Special Forces, from The John F. Kennedy Special Warfare Center and School. The school is made up of nearly one hundred permanent instructors, from all services, who annually train approximately one thousand students from all the military services in free-fall parachute techniques.

According to GlobalSecurity.com:

"MFF team members are taught to conduct operational high-altitude, low-opening (HALO) missions by exiting an aircraft at altitudes up to 35,000 feet above ground level. The MFF parachutists free fall to about 2,500 feet from ground level before deploying their canopies. During high-altitude, high-opening, (HAHO), parachute missions, MFF para-

chutists exit at high altitudes and deploy their canopies at high altitudes using highly maneuverable, gliding parachute systems to silently travel distances of more than 50 kilometers.

"[The course is] taught at Fort Bragg, North Carolina, and Yuma Proving Ground, Arizona. During the first week, called ground week, students learn body stabilization while flying in the vertical wind tunnel at Fort Bragg as well as basic aircraft procedures, altitude physiology, and other MFF parachuting ground training.

"Students go to Yuma Proving Ground for their airborne operations during the last two weeks. Advanced aircraft procedures beginning with individual exits while wearing combat equipment introduce students to the MFF infiltration mission. Students learn mass exits, grouping exercises, night airborne operations, and high-altitude airborne procedures in combat equipment and oxygen gear."

Military free-fall operations are generally characterized by flight over or adjacent to the objective area at altitudes not normally associated with conventional parachute operations. Ram-air parachuted and supplemental oxygen permit long-range surveillance detachment (LRSD) members to exit the aircraft with maximum standoff, deploy their parachutes at a designated altitude, assemble in the air, and land together on the drop zone. Military free-fall operations can be conducted except under the most adverse weather conditions.

As GlobalSecurity.org explains:

"High-altitude airdrop missions (HAAMS) for special-assignment airlift missions (SAAMS), often top-secret and clandestine affairs, carry elite troops from every branch of the service: U.S. Army Rangers and Special Forces, Marine Recon forces, navy SEAL teams, and air force special tactics units. Jumpers from all services parachute at altitudes up to 35,000 feet with all of the accompanying hazards. High-glide-ratio parachutes (HGRP) utilize high-altitude low-opening (HALO) and high-altitude high-opening (HAHO) techniques during day and night operations and under all weather conditions.

"The HALO techniques are used for missions to prevent detection of the aircraft and the jumpers. Extreme accuracy is required since the parachutes are deployed at a low altitude. HALO involves paratroopers jumping at around 25,000 feet and freefalling down to 3,500 feet. Plummeting at a terminal velocity of 126 mph, parachutists can descend this distance within two minutes. A HALO jump gets the jumper out of sight in a hurry, and they are less vulnerable to dangers. A drawback to this technique is that the jumpers must exit the aircraft over, or close to, enemy territory, thus making the aircraft a potential target for enemy surface-to-air or air-to-air defenses.

"The HAHO techniques are used for missions [that] require minimal detection of the aircraft under conditions which restrict the aircraft from penetrating a certain area, such as the border of a country. The jumpers will deploy the parachutes at very high altitudes, which allow them to glide a considerable horizontal distance with a low probability of detection. Jumpers are consequently exposed to hypoxia and cold temperatures for extended periods. A HAHO is a high-altitude, high-opening jump used for long-range insertion. During high-altitude, high-opening missions both exit and deployment altitudes

are high, and a special parachute lets them maneuver more than 50 kilometers as they quietly float into an area. HAHO allows the jump aircraft to deliver its cargo from a significant standoff range, thereby reducing the odds of enemy detection and increasing the survivability of the aircraft and the parachutists. The higher the parachute-opening altitude and the flatter the glide slope of the parachute, the greater the standoff distance attainable. Paratroopers 'hop and pop' their 'chutes' immediately, which is potentially a riskier maneuver because jumpers are exposed to altitude and the enemy for a longer period. The opening shock is also traumatic. It gives quite a jolt. Jumpers are sore for a few days after a HAHO.

"Given the same size parachutes, a heavier parachutist will descend more rapidly than a lighter one. This variable rate of descent is not a problem in low-altitude airborne work; military parachutists traditionally carry their individual combat gear with little regard for weight considerations. However, that approach doesn't work in HAHO operations. Because a HAHO team may travel more than 40 miles under their canopies, a common rate of descent is a critical factor in keeping the team together. To ensure the glide slopes are as uniform as possible, the team's gear is carefully apportioned so that all the team members weigh about the same—heavier troops jump with lighter equipment containers; lighter troops jump with heavier containers. The team's equipment can be redistributed into operational loads after landing. . . .

"Decompression sickness (DCS) is an illness caused by hypobaric (reduced atmospheric) pressure on the body that results in production of nitrogen bubbles within body tissues, similar to bends. These bubbles result in symptoms of DCS, which can cause mild joint pain to right ventricular failure and circulatory collapse, to permanent neurological deficits (paraplegia), and to death. Above 21,000 feet pressure altitude, potentially lethal DCS is a virtual certainty unless oxygen discipline is strictly followed and all oxygen equipment functions adequately. Increased time at high altitude greatly contributes to an incidence of DCS due to growth of nitrogen bubbles formation. Thus personnel exposed to high altitude should be discouraged from strenuous exercise immediately after exposure such as combat operations for twelve hours post-flight."

Ira Hayes was one of six men who raised the flag on Iwo Jima in the famous photograph. He was a paramarine (marine paratrooper) assigned to a marine infantry unit during World War II.

and these multiply as you go higher. At thirty-five thousand feet, you'll have between thirty to sixty seconds of useful consciousness without supplemental oxygen. Ultimately, this leads to death."

U.S. MARINE CORPS PARACHUTE OPERATIONS

The Marine Corps has been involved in parachute operations since World War II, though in a much smaller scale than the army. During World War II, the marines formed a parachute regiment with four parachute battalions. These "paramarines" were never employed in large-scale airborne operations, and the regiment was disbanded by 1944 and the marines dispersed to infantry regiments. One of the most famous of the airborne marines was Ira Hayes, one of six flag raisers on Mt. Suribachi, Iwo Jima.

Since World War II, the majority of marines who have attended BAC have been in the reconnaissance community, and most of those have been from Force Reconnaissance. Force Recon marines have earned a reputation for superhuman physical endurance and expertise in fieldcraft.

In 2006, the 2nd Force Reconnaissance Battalion was deactivated and replaced by the 2nd Marine Special Operations Battalion (MSOB), the second unit to be formed under the newly created Marine Corps Forces Special Operations Command. The 2nd MSOB is located at Camp Lejeune, North Carolina, and will consist of five companies. A similar organization, the 1st MSOB, is planned for Camp Pendleton, California. This reorganization recognizes the evolution of Force Recon into a key element of the special operations community.

In addition to members of the reconnaissance community, the marine corps sends air and naval gunfire liaison specialists, parachute riggers, and air-delivery specialists to the Basic Airborne Course.

Marine and navy parachutists wear the navy parachutist badge once they qualify. The navy wings are easily distinguished from the army wings, or "lead sled," by its gold color and spread wings. In order to qualify for navy wings, a marine must be in a jump billet and make an additional five jumps from a navy aircraft after the completion of the Basic Airborne Course. Two of the five jumps must be night jumps, one with combat equipment. Some marines can spend a year chasing their gold wings and are often on the receiving end of mild hazing by those who have already qualified.

The two greatest hazards they must contend with on high-altitude air-drop missions, HAAMS for short, are hypoxia and decompression sickness. Decompression sickness, or the bends, occurs when nitrogen bubbles form in the blood and tissues after a rapid reduction in surrounding pressure. It's manifested by pain in the joints and is potentially lethal.

Hypoxia is a major concern during both techniques; there is one documented fatality associated with a high-altitude jump. According to an article in the July 1997 issue of *Airman* magazine, "Oxygen deprivation causes hypoxia, and its symptoms include dizziness, giddiness, a tingling sensation, euphoria, blurred or tunnel vision, lack of muscle coordination, and slow reaction time. To compensate for the body's craving for oxygen, the heart and breathing rate increases." The article quoted Tech. Sgt. Don Blackwell, an aerospace physiology technician, "Hypoxia affects people uniquely, and its symptoms will change with age and lifestyle. That's why all aircrew members are required to go through the [altitude] chamber regularly." Further, the article quoted Lt. Col. Don Flanagan, Air Combat Command physiologist, "At ten thousand feet, subtle changes take place in the body

U.S. NAVY PARACHUTE OPERATIONS

According to GlobalSecurity.org, it is the mission of the commander, Naval Special Warfare Command (COMNAVSPECWARCOM), to "prepare Naval Special Warfare (NSW) forces to carry out assigned missions and to develop maritime special operations strategy, doctrine, and tactics. COMNAVSPECWARCOM exercises operational control over all United States-based Naval Special Warfare Command training, operational control of all United States-based Naval Special Warfare forces, and responsibility for the training, equipping, supporting, and providing trained and ready forces to the combatant commanders." Sailors from other fields also attend BAC, from specialties such as explosive ordnance disposal and aircrew survival specialists.

U.S. Navy SEALs get most of the attention in the naval special warfare community. The selection and training of candidates at Basic Underwater Demolition School (BUDS) is justifiably considered some of the most difficult military training in the world. Airborne qualification is a basic requirement to be a SEAL. SEALs are extremely active in the Global War on Terror, usually engaged in the most dangerous unconventional warfare missions.

As GlobalSecurity.org explains:

"A tactical force with strategic impact, Naval Special Warfare (NSW) mission areas include unconventional warfare, direct action, combating terrorism, special reconnaissance, foreign internal defense, information warfare, security assistance, counterdrug operations, personnel recovery, and hydrographic reconnaissance. NSW forces can operate independently or integrate with other U.S. special operations forces or within U.S. Navy carrier battle groups and amphibious ready groups.

"Naval special warfare units are organized, trained, and equipped to conduct special operations in maritime and riverine environments. They are deployed in small units worldwide in support of fleet and national operations. NSW provides an effective means to apply counterforce in conjunction with national policy and objectives in peacetime and across the spectrum of hostilities from peacetime operations to limited war to general war."

U.S. AIR FORCE PARACHUTE OPERATIONS

U.S. Air Force Special Operations has the mission to provide the air component of U.S. Special Operations Command, deploying specialized airpower and delivering special operations combat power. This includes units that provide direct action, unconventional warfare, special reconnaissance, foreign internal defense, and counter-terrorism support to unified commands.

According to GlobalSecurity.org:

"Combat controllers, pararescue, and combat weather make up Air Force Special Tactics, one of the most highly trained and versatile specialties in the Department of Defense. For those looking to earn the scarlet beret, they can expect two years of some of the most challenging training in the U.S. military. They will be well-rounded, highly skilled warriors after they attend Air Traffic Control School, Army Airborne School, Survival School, Combat Control School, Scuba School, and High Altitude Low Opening Jump School. The toughest career in the air force, combat controllers (CCTs), is a small force of fewer than four hundred men.

"In the army, it's the rangers. In the navy, it's the SEALs. In the air force, it's combat control. As proved in Grenada, Panama, and Iraq, successful military operations often require combat controllers to be 'first there.' They are ground combat forces assigned to special tactics squadrons within the Air Force Special Operations Command (AFSOC). They are organized, trained, and equipped to rapidly establish and control the air-ground interface and provide airmanship skills in the objective area. Their functions include assault zone assessment and establishment; air traffic control; command and control communications; special operations terminal attack control; and removal of obstacles and unexploded ordnance with demolitions. They provide a unique capability and deploy with joint air and ground forces in the execution of direct action, counterterrorism, foreign internal defense, humanitarian assistance, special reconnaissance, austere airfield and combat search-and-rescue operations.

"Air force combat controller[s are] trained to infiltrate hostile areas and provide ground forces, aircraft, and headquarters commanders with vital satellite communications, command, and control links. They usually carry approximately one hundred pounds of equipment consisting of weapons, night-vision goggles, oxygen equipment for high-altitude parachuting, rappelling equipment, state-of-the-art communications equipment, and anything else needed to complete the mission.

"The 720th Special Tactics Group, with headquarters at Hurlburt Field, Florida, has special operations combat controllers, pararescuemen, and combat weathermen who work jointly in special tactics teams (STT). It provides intermediate command, control and coordination for air force special tactics forces deployed worldwide. These forces comprise combat controllers and pararescuemen who form fast-action deployable units in support of joint or combined special operations task forces.

"There are six special tactics squadrons (STS) and one combat weather squadron; all of which, except the 320th and 321st STS, fall under the direct command and control of the 720th STG. The 320th STS at Kadena Air Base, Japan, and the 320th STS at RAF Mildenhall, England, are assigned to and under the operational control of the 353rd and the 352nd Special Operations Groups respectively, but under the functional management of the 720th STG.

"The 720th also includes the 10th Combat Weather Squadron with headquarters at Hurlburt Field, Florida, and detachments co-located with U.S. Army Special Operations Command units.

"The mission of the 720th Special Tactics Group is to organize, train, and equip special tactics forces world-wide to establish and control the air-ground interface during special operations missions by conducting airfield or assault zone reconnaissance, assessment, and control; and providing immediate emergency trauma medical treatment and patient retrieval as well as combat search-and-rescue when directed.

U.S. Air Force pararescuemen from the 31st Rescue Squadron perform a static-line jump out of a C-130 Hercules aircraft over a body of water near Kadena Air Base, Japan, August 29, 2006. The 18th Wing and the 353rd Special Operations Group are conducting a mass-casualty exercise to test the rescue and emergency care capabilities of Kadena Air Base.
Department of Defense photo by Staff Sgt. Steven Nabor, U.S. Air Force

U.S. Air Force pararescuemen from the 58th Rescue Squadron and combat controllers from the 414th Combat Training Squadron, Nellis Air Force Base, Nevada, jump from a C-130J Hercules aircraft. This jump took place on September 1, 2006 over Lake Mead in support of exercise Red Flag 06-2. *U.S. Air Force photo by Master Sgt. Kevin J. Gruenwald*

"The 720th STG also provides long-range operational and logistics planning and deploys command and control elements during special tactics force employment or deployment. Lastly, it functions as the command's proponent for military parachuting, diving, and other special tactics related matters.

"These forces also position navigational aids and target designation equipment and control offensive fire systems, either in permissive or hostile environments.

"The 720th STG ensures special tactics forces are organized, trained, and equipped to provide a combat ready force. This includes utilization of mission-unique skills involving parachuting techniques of low-altitude static line, free-fall high-altitude low-opening (HALO), and high-altitude high-opening (HAHO) procedures. . . ."

Perhaps the best known of air force special operations personnel are the pararescuemen, or PJs. They have the distinction of being the only group specifically trained and equipped to conduct conventional or unconventional rescue operations in the U.S. armed forces.

The PJs are highly trained, with nearly two years of schooling required before they are considered proficient in their trade. In addition to training in methods of infiltration and survival, they spend nearly a year learning emergency medical skills. They are rated among the best emergency trauma specialists in the Department of Defense. A high level of intelligence and physical fitness are required to be a PJ.

Their motto, "That Others May Live," reflects not only the high quality of their training but that they are willing to sacrifice their own lives while saving others. This motto has been put to the test thousands of times,

Paratroopers from the 1st Battalion (Airborne), 507th Infantry, relax before loading onto C-17A Globemaster III cargo aircraft. They will be part of a sixteen-aircraft paratroop drop celebrating the sixtieth anniversary of the D-day Normandy Invasion during World War II.

and many thousands are alive today thanks to the PJs.

The PJs' primary mission is personnel recovery, with emergency medical capabilities in humanitarian and combat environments. They can deploy a combat search-and-rescue capability in any available manner—by air, land, or sea—into restricted environments to authenticate, extract, treat, stabilize, and evacuate injured personnel, while acting in an enemy-evading, recovery role. Pararescuemen also provide recovery support for NASA and conduct other operations, such as humanitarian rescue, as appropriate.

CONCLUSION

Jump wings are more than just a badge signifying the completion of a course of military instruction. They are an intangible bond with heroes past, membership in a brotherhood forged in fire and tempered in sacrifice, and symbolic of a tradition of courage. Wear them with pride.

Index

Index of Units

1st Cavalry Division, 85

1st Special Forces Operational Detacment (Airborne): Delta Force, 130, 131

1st Special Warfare Training Group, 130

2nd Marine Special Operations Battalion, 136

3rd Brigade, 9

3rd Infantry Division (Mechanized), 9

3rd Ranger Battalion, 17

B Company, 17

C Company, 18

4th Reconnaissance Company, 129

11th Airborne Division, 17

17th Airborne Division, 15

31st Rescue Squadron, (USAF), 139

41st Rescue Squadron (USAF), 125

58th Rescue Squadron (USAF), 140

66th Rescue Squadron (USAF), 127

75th Ranger Regiment, 9, 17, 124–127

1st Battalion, 124

2nd Battalion, 124

3rd Battalion, 124

Ranger Course, 124

Ranger Training Brigade, 124

82nd Airborne Division, 14, 15, 17, 121, 122, 124, 131

509th Parachute Infantry Battalion (PIB), 14

1st Battalion, 19

XVIII Airborne Corps, 122, 131

101st Airborne Division, 14, 15, 17, 21, 122, 123

173rd Airborne Brigade, 17, 18, 122

187th Regimental Combat Team, 17

414th Combat Training Squadron, 140

503rd Parachute Battalion, 14, 17, 18, 20, 21

A Company, 13

504th Parachute Infantry Regiment, 2nd Battalion, 17

507th Infantry, 108

1st Battalion, 10, 31, 126, 141

Index of Aircraft

Boeing C-17A Globemaster III, 121

CH-53 Sea Stallion, 129

Douglas C-33, 14

Douglas C-47, 14, 18

Lockheed C-130 Hercules, 22, 38, 61, 62, 66, 83, 86, 88, 105, 110, 125, 132, 138, 139, 108

C-130J, 140

HC-130, 127

Lockheed C-141 Starlifter cargo transport, 87, 126, 132

Lockheed C-17, 38, 61, 132

C-17A Globemaster III, 108, 62, 86, 141

Lockheed C-5, 132

MC-130E Combat Talon I, 120

General Index

A Bridge Too Far, 15

ADEPT method, 85, 86, 114

Advanced parachute training schools, 131–136

Advanced Airborne School, 131

Jumpmaster School, 132

Military Free Fall School, 132–136

Pathfinder School, 132

Adverse weather aerial delivery system (AWADS), 95

Airborne School, 9

Airborne Walk, 118

ALICE pack, 69, 74, 85, 86, 106, 107

Army Physical Fitness Test (APFT), 24, 35, 38–43, 129, 132

Basic Airborne Course (BAC), 9, 10, 23–119, 121

Arrival, 29

Ground week, 36–57

Airborne orientation, 41

Entrance exam, 38–41

Five points of performance, 46, 47

Methods of recovery, 54

Mock-door training/actions inside aircraft, 47–49

Parachute landing falls (PLFs), 52–57

PT schedule, 42, 43

Summary, 57

Thirty-four-foot tower, 50, 51

In-processing, 31, 32

Jump week, 80–119

Jump schedule, 85

Jumpmaster personnel inspections (JMPI), 96–102

Operation briefing, 88, 92

Out the door, 110–115

Rigging combat equipment for parachuting, 85, 86

Static-line parachuting, 86–88

Sustained airborne training, 92–96

Packing list, 27, 28

Prerequisites, 26

Reporting guidelines, 32

Roster number, 32

Tower week, 58–79

250-foot tower, 73

Common errors, 69, 70

Mock-door training, 62–68

Parachute malfunctions, 73–79

PT schedule, 61

Suspended-harness training, 70–72

Swing-landing trainer, 72, 73

Thirty-four-foot tower, 67–69

Beckwith, Col. Charles, 130

Benning, Henry L., 9

Black Hats, 33–35

Blackwell, Tech. Sgt. Don, 136

Camp MacKall, 130

Caserma Ederle, Italy, 122

Drop zone safety officer (DZSO), 34

Eberhart, Pvt. Aubrey, 18
Eubanks Field, 10, 41, 50, 73, 118

Fallschirmjägers (German
paratroopers), 11, 14
Financial fitness, 27
Flanagan, Lt. Col. Don, 136
Flexed-arm hang text, 38, 39
Fort Benning, 9, 10, 14, 21, 23, 24, 29,
    35, 37, 41, 47, 57, 73, 82, 98, 108, 118,
    119, 121, 124, 126, 131, 132
Fort Bragg, 10, 121, 122, 130–132
Fort Campbell, 122
Fort Kelly, 11
Fort Lewis, 124
Fort Stewart, 124
Franklin, Benjamin, 11
Fryar Drop Zone, 34, 81–83, 86, 87,
    108, 112–114, 117, 118

Geronimo (Goyathlay), 18
Ground Branch, 50

Hayes, Ira, 136
Howard, 1st Sgt. Ed, 73

India Program, 38

John F. Kennedy Special Warfare Center
    and School, 134
Johnson, President Lyndon B., 17
Jump boots, 20
Jump wings, 20, 21
Jumpmaster personnel inspection
    (JMPI), 32, 63, 82, 89

King, Pvt. William "Red," 14
Korean War, 17

Lawson Army Airfield, 14, 22, 82, 88, 98

McCarthy Hall, 82, 88, 89, 92, 98, 102,
    104–106
Mitchell, Gen. William "Billy," 11

Nicholas, Adrian, 11

Operation Enduring Freedom, 17
Operation Iraqi Freedom, 18
Operation Overlord (D-day, June 6,
    1944), 14

Patton, Gen., 15
Physical Fitness Training, 41, 43, 61
Physical training, 24–26

Ranger Training Brigade, 9
Ryder, 1st Lt. William T., 14
School of the Americas, 9

Silver Wings, 118
Simpson, Pvt. Leroy F., 21
Simpson, Pvt. Thomas L., 21
Special Forces Assessment and
Selection Course (SFAS), 130
Special Forces Qualification Course
    (SFQC), 130
Static Line Parachuting Techniques and
    Training, 38, 54, 62, 82

T10 parachute, 44, 45, 82, 97
Test Platoon, 14, 21
Third Army, 15
Tower Branch, 50

U.S. Air Force, 108, 110, 120, 132
Parachute operations, 137–141
U.S. Army airborne divisions and
    brigades, 122, 123
U.S. Army Airborne, 18
U.S. Army Infantry Training Brigade, 9
U.S. Army John F. Kennedy Special
    Warfare Center and School, 130
U.S. Army National Guard, 127, 130
U.S. Army Reserve, 130
U.S. Army Special Force Command
    (Airborne): Green Berets, 127–130
U.S. Infantry School, 9
U.S. Marine Corps, 132
Parachute operations, 136
U.S. Navy, Parachute operations, 137
U.S. Navy SEAL, 120, 131, 133, 137
Uniform Code of Military Justice
    (UCMJ), 29, 57

Vietnam War, 17

Weart, Col. Steve, 17
Wilson, Gen. James, 9
World War II, 14–17

Yarborough, Capt. William, 20, 21

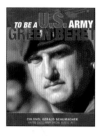

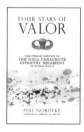
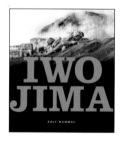
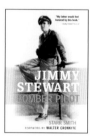